T0348400

Investment performance measurement

Investment performance measurement

WILLIAM G BAIN

in association with The WM Company

WOODHEAD PUBLISHING LIMITED

Cambridge England

Published by Woodhead Publishing Ltd
Abington Hall, Abington
Cambridge CB1 6AH, England

First published 1996, Woodhead Publishing Ltd

British Library Cataloguing in Publication Data
A catalogue record for this book is available from the British Library.

ISBN 1 85573 195 9

Contents

Foreword

Given the interest in investment returns by individuals, corporations and institutional funds, it is surprising that there is little literature on the development, the rationale, the calculation methods and the use of investment performance measurement and analysis. *Investment Performance Measurement* fills this gap for both the layman and the professional.

The measurement and analysis of investment performance results can be quite confusing and is often different and inconsistent in its presentation. This book, therefore, provides a timely insight into the practice and mathematics of a subject which affects more and more people, either through their individual savings or through collective schemes such as insurance or pension funds. They will find much to enlighten them. For the professional investor the history is relevant, but much more important are the examples of calculations of returns and attribution. Risk is reviewed and explained, together with the reasons why its use is relatively limited – universal acceptance is some distance away.

With more investors making better use of stock market indices, and with the development of customised benchmarks, this book provides all the necessary background information to keep control of one's investments. There are also signposts to what is possible as advances in technology, communications and data handling allow for greater analysis and insight into performance results.

This book provides essential information to readers at all levels. The private investor, the student, the investment manager and the consultant will all find rewards in its pages.

Philip Lambert
Chairman, NAPF Performance Monitoring Group

Preface

What is a book on 'performance measurement' expected to be about? When asked to prepare such a book I decided to investigate what other material was available on the subject. A search through the university libraries databank using the two key words threw up a mass of references; unfortunately most of them were concerned with manufacturing industry, production performance or engineering! It rapidly became clear that the qualifications 'investment' or 'portfolio' had to be incorporated.

This book is therefore concerned with the measurement and analysis of the investment performance of portfolios and funds. Moreover the main emphasis, particularly in the examples used, is on pension funds. This is mainly because they represent a large and diverse pool of assets with a broadly common objective – to build up a fund of financial assets which will meet the future liability to provide retirement pensions to the underlying subscribers.

Moreover the need for accountability to the members has encouraged pension funds to measure their performance in a consistent manner and to report to their members. As a result a reasonable body of historic data is available.

In structuring the book I have first looked at the historical development of performance measurement. Despite the very long history of investment, including investment in publicly quoted securities, the process of systematic measurement of performance (not to be confused with valuation) is relatively new. It emerged in a formal way only in the 1960s but has developed rapidly since then.

Although apparently simple and straightforward, the process of performance measurement is fraught with problems and the second section of the book deals with the practical aspects of measurement and analysis. In this section the layman may find the reasons why the same portfolio may have a different valuation and calculated return when measured by two different bodies. Although this section contains some detailed examples it keeps separate the two aspects of performance measurement – return and risk – with a separate chapter devoted to each. It may therefore offer a different insight to that provided by most textbooks on the subject.

In Section Three I have drawn on available data to illustrate the results achieved by pension funds over the twenty years 1975–94 and some of the characteristics of investment returns that analysis of the data has highlighted.

Finally, I have looked at current developments and speculated on where they might lead by the next millennium.

But why prepare such a book?

During the past several years as a consultant at The WM Company I have been asked, and had to provide the answers to, various questions about performance measurement and have been surprised at the lack of readily available material. The last broad reference book on the subject was published in 1980[1] and much has happened over the intervening period. The investment process has become more international, investment instruments have become more complex and participants have become more interested in understanding something which can be crucial to their future welfare.

It had become clear that there was scope to produce a book which would provide answers to many of the questions posed by professionals and lay persons alike in one convenient source. As a result I have aimed the book at a broad spectrum of reader. Some of the chapters contain straightforward information, others are of a more technical nature. In these instances I have had to rely on the considerable expertise of my colleagues at The WM Company whose knowledge of the algebra and the algorithms involved in index construction and performance calculations far exceeds my own. Plan sponsors and trustees of pension funds should find the descriptive chapters helpful in understanding the complexities of performance measurement but there is also sufficient technical description to assist students and practitioners, such as fund managers and consultants, to come to terms with both the process and the outcome of performance measurement and analysis.

Inevitably I have drawn heavily on the material available to me at The WM Company but where possible I have also cited examples from elsewhere, including the USA and Europe. The material should therefore be of interest and value to readers, not only in the UK but also in the USA, Europe or, indeed, anywhere that performance measurement of investment funds is practised or contemplated, since much of the content is universal in its relevance and application.

---

[1] 'The measurement of portfolio performance', Clifford Hymans and John Mulligan, Kluwer Publishing Ltd, 1980.

Acknowledgements

Firstly I would like to thank Dugald Eadie for persuading me to become involved in this exercise in the first place and for his help in producing the initial framework document. Also to The WM Company for encouragement and financial support including access to much of their extensive databank and library of material. Without their combined intervention I would not have undertaken the task.

Having commenced, I owe thanks to many colleagues within The WM Company but particularly to Ian Haddow, Robert Darling and Douglas Brown for their work on Chapters 5 and 8 respectively. Gordon Bagot has also undertaken the role of supervising much of my work and offering editorial support.

Special thanks must go to the people who have undertaken the physical task of producing the manuscript. To Joan Pryde and subsequently to Karen Stevens and Julie Gallagher, for typing the manuscript and many of the tables of truly daunting complexity. Jon Dalrymple and Sandra Murphy have also added their expertise in assembling the data for tables and charts in a form which would be acceptable to the publishers and Stuart Clelland solved the problem of producing an index. Also to many others at The WM Company who offered their comments and items of information relevant to their own areas of expertise, I extend my thanks.

John Gillies at Frank Russell Company and David Wilkie at R Watson & Sons were generous in their support in reading and commenting on early drafts and I extend my especial thanks to them. Other organisations have also been helpful in allowing reproduction of material from their various reports and publications.

Finally my thanks to Neil Wenborn for his patience in waiting for the final manuscript, and to Tina for her encouragement and understanding when things did not run as smoothly as I might have hoped.

What is performance measurement?

Performance
- a piece of work.

- manner or success in working.

- instance of awkward, aggressive, embarrassing behaviour (coll.)!

Measure
- the ascertainment of extent by comparison with a standard.
(Source: Chambers English Dictionary)

That there is a need to establish a value for an asset has not been questioned since the advent of accountancy. Portfolio investments, as with other assets, were valued periodically in order to establish the balance sheet of assets and liabilities. The valuation thus provided vital information to the accountant and, ultimately, to the owner or custodian of the asset.

Consecutive valuations added further information by establishing a pattern or trend in the value of the assets; whether they were rising or falling in value.

Performance measurement implies much more than simply a valuation for accounting purposes, even if the valuations are made over successive periods. The implication is one of judgement, of satisfaction, and comparison with a standard or target of attainment. It implies the exercise of management control for the purposes of analysis, for decision taking and action.

Unless those elements are implicit in the process then performance measurement is a waste of time and resources. A simple valuation and balance sheet statement would suffice to inform interested parties whether or not a pension fund, for example, was viable, or an insurance fund was solvent.

This section will examine those elements in the process which differentiate valuation from performance.

Chapter 1 looks at the development of the concepts of performance measurement as experienced in the USA and the UK. The evolution of

1

benchmarks either in the form of indices or of peer group universes is covered in Chapter 2. The development of the analysis of performance data and the increasing sophistication as data handling systems improved appears in Chapter 3. The section concludes with a review of how the information is utilised in the exercise of management control both by the day to day managers of the assets and by the ultimate custodians of responsibility for the assets.

History of performance measurement

Introduction

Prior to the 1960s it had been generally accepted that a straightforward valuation of assets which could be compared with a similar valuation at an earlier date was sufficient information for the owner of the assets. For a more sophisticated level of information a comparison might be made with a benchmark – usually the most widely used index relevant to the asset.

With the competitive claims of asset managers, particularly in the area of publicly promoted mutual funds or unit trusts, came the need to make more effective assessments of the management of assets. Such assessments needed a more rigorous approach to the problem of performance measurement in order to make proper comparisons.

This chapter provides a brief resumé of the evolution of this process through the 1960s and 1970s in the USA and the UK.

Early development in the USA

It is difficult to establish when the process of simply producing asset valuations moved on to one of measuring performance as currently defined. The earliest manifestation occurs in work dealing with funds in the public domain – unit trusts (in the UK) or mutual funds (in the USA). Because these funds produced a regular valuation of assets and a unitised price to accommodate cash flows into or out of the fund they were an obvious choice for analysis. In the USA, in particular, services which monitored the price changes in mutual funds and ranked their price performance over various time periods were being published in the 1950s. Changes in the level of the Standard and Poor's Index would also be monitored as a basis of comparison.

These funds were thus subject to, at least, some form of performance measurement albeit of limited value in assessing the relative merits of the management of those funds. For although they were usually equity funds invested in the US market they were far from being homogeneous.

This problem was recognised in the Wharton report – *A Study of Mutual Funds* – published in 1962. That report, which analysed the performance of investment funds in the fifties recognised that the specific market conditions at the time would have influenced the results of the funds which had quite different characteristics. A simple comparison of price performance would not necessarily provide a satisfactory indicator of relative management performance.

In addressing this problem, of comparing funds of different structures, Jack L Treynor published a keynote paper in the Harvard Business Review in 1965.[1] That paper suggested a methodology for comparing the performance of the different funds' management. Rates of return (capital change plus income) were used to construct 'market characteristic lines'. Although the slope of these lines might vary under different market conditions the ranking of different funds by characteristic line did not vary. The impact of management rather than market conditions could thus be assessed. In effect Treynor was adjusting the observed returns on the funds by the market impact and the fund's sensitivity to the market. This aspect of volatility or riskiness was later to appear as Beta in risk adjusted returns. (See Chapter 8 Risk.)

At around the same time that the Treynor paper was published, A G Becker and Co Inc (a Chicago based investment banking firm) were considering the problem of assessing the performance of their clients' pension fund managers. They were aware that such measurement methods as were employed were so diverse as to make comparisons very difficult, if not meaningless. They realised that if meaningful results were to be obtained they had to establish a formalised approach to measuring performance and a standard or standards with which it might be compared.

Such was their success in tackling this problem that Becker were able to launch their Funds Evaluation Service aimed at the retirement funds of corporations and other bodies and within a short time had established a databank of such funds which could be used for comparative purposes.

Before real inter-fund comparisons could be made, however, a methodology for taking account of the timing of money flows into and out of the fund had to be devised. P O Dietz made an important contribution on this subject in his

---

[1] 'How to Rate Management of Investment Funds', Jack L Treynor, *Harvard Business Review*, Jan/Feb 1965.

work published in 1966.[2]   This contained the first comprehensive introduction to the concept of Time Weighted Returns (TWR).

The Bank Administration Institute (BAI) had started a research project in 1965 to develop an improved method of measuring the performance of pension funds.   The project had two broad objectives: 'First, it was hoped that the method developed would be adopted generally by banks and their customers, thereby permitting valid comparisons of results achieved by different pension funds and by different pension fund managers.   Second, it was hoped that the principles of measurement identified in the project ultimately could be extended to other types of portfolios managed by banks'.[3]   The report containing the results of this project was published by the BAI in December 1968 and laid the foundations for a systematic and consistent approach to performance measurement in the USA.

The following is a summary of the main recommendations of that report.

1.   *The performance of pension funds should be measured in two dimensions: rate of return and risk.*

2.   *Rates of return should be based on income and on changes in the market value of assets held.   Both the time-weighted rate of return and the internal rate of return should be computed.   The time-weighted rate of return measures the results of investment decisions made by a fund manager.   It is not affected by decisions about the timing and amounts of cash flows – decisions which the fund manager typically does not make.   The internal rate of return measures a fund's total investment performance, regardless of the source of decision-making, and is helpful in determining the adequacy of the fund to meets its obligations.   Rates of return should be expressed as annual rates, compounded annually.*

3.   *Rates of return should be calculated for calendar quarters as well as for longer periods of time.   Performance comparisons for longer periods are the more important comparisons.*

4.   *Until future research indicates a better way, it is recommended at the outset that the degree of risk taken in a fund be estimated by calculating the mean absolute deviation of the time-weighted rate of return.   Such calculation should be based on quarterly rates of return beginning with the start of the process of systematic evaluation.*

---

[2] *Pension Funds: Measuring Investment Performance*, P O Dietz, The Free Press, 1966.
[3] *Measuring Investment Performance of Pension Funds*, Bank Administration Institute, December 1988.

5. *The most important measures of rates of return and of risk are those relating to total portfolios. For diagnostic purposes, however, it will be useful to have measures of performance for the following classes of assets:*

- *Common stocks and warrants.*

- *Assets convertible into common stocks.*

- *Cash and temporary investments, including all fixed income investments with less than one year to maturity from the date of valuation.*

- *Intermediate and long range fixed income assets.*

- *Assets purchased or held at the direction of the trustor.*

- *Other (such as real estate and commodities).*

6. *Since it is believed that inter-fund comparisons will be more valuable if there is a pooling of data for funds administered by different managers, it is recommended that plans be developed for collecting such data from banks and that the analysis of pooled data be made available to participating banks.*

Development in the UK

In the UK, in a paper published in 1962,[4] A B Gilliland acknowledged that for a closed fund the growth in capital value and income could be monitored over time and compared with a chosen benchmark. He commented that the great majority of portfolios were not of fixed amount, however, and the effect of new money complicates the evaluation of performance. He suggested a method of constructing a 'Capital Index' and an 'Income Index' for any fund which could then be compared with any chosen yardstick.

The 'Capital Index' was constructed using the periodic market values of the portfolio, say quarterly, after subtracting the value of net new money invested during the quarter, adjusted for the movement in the benchmark index and allowing for investment costs. In practice, the net new money was assumed to be invested evenly over the period so the numerator of the adjustment factor equalled one half of the movement in the benchmark index. Thus Gilliland's paper pre-dated the eventual recommendation to use a time weighted return as proposed by Dietz.

---

[4] 'Measuring Ordinary Share Portfolio Performance', *The Investment Analyst*, August 1962. A B Gilliland, Investment Manager, Philips Pension Funds.

The subject of performance measurement was also discussed at the third congress of the European Federation of Financial Analysts at Knokke in Belgium in January 1965. In February 1972 the Society of Investment Analysts (SIA)[5] in the UK published its own report on 'The Measurement of Portfolio Performance for Pension Funds' as prepared by a working group under the chairmanship of M G Hall.

The following is the summary of that paper.

The subject of portfolio performance measurement for pension funds has been receiving increasing attention in recent years, particularly since the publication in October 1968 in the USA of the Bank Administration Institute (BAI) report on this subject. Towards the end of 1970 a working group was set up by the Society of Investment Analysts to make recommendations on this subject and this report specifically puts forward methods of calculating portfolio performance figures, thus making possible a general comparison between funds.

The approach recommended has as its twin aims the calculation of a rate of return with which to compare funds and the analysis of the performance of a fund into two components – selection of stocks and selection of sectors. The first aim is achieved by calculation of the Time Weighted Return using a comparatively simple approximation which it is believed will normally be accurate enough for most purposes. The analysis of performance is produced by constructing notional funds based on market indices and comparing these with the actual fund. This analysis will, it is felt, be vitally important in identifying the importance of the various investment decisions.

The report includes sections dealing with the selection of indices for the notional funds, expenses and the collection of data. A worked example is described in full. The calculations needed in the tests are quite straightforward and simple to perform manually but they are also particularly suitable for carrying out using a computer terminal.

Finally it is recommended that the test should preferably be carried out at quarterly intervals and that a measure of the variability of the time-weighted returns and performance figures should be calculated so that over a three to five year period, the significance of the average figure may be judged.

As with the BAI, the paper emphasised the need for the calculation of the time weighted return if comparison between funds was to be valid.

Both the BAI and the IIMR recognised that the TWR was an approximation unless an accurate valuation of the fund was obtained at the time of every cash

---

[5] The SIA later became the Institute for Investment Management and Research (IIMR) and will be referred to as such throughout the remainder of the book.

flow. (This would be very impractical although mutual funds or unit trusts do carry out daily, or more frequent, valuations in order to calculate unit prices for transaction purposes.) In practice most measurement systems use monthly valuations with an assumption about the timing of cash flows within the month – usually the middle of the month. If cash flows are significant and lumpy it is usual to take special note and in many cases a valuation on the specified day would be required.

For more detail on the TWR and the MWR see Chapter 5.

Risk

The BAI and the IIMR also recognised the significance of risk but there were some differences between the two countries in the extent to which the treatment recommended was adopted. The BAI recommended measuring risk by calculating the total variability of TWRs over specified time intervals, and the IIMR accepted that, although not a fully satisfactory method of measuring risk, the mean absolute deviation of TWRs was recommended as an acceptable proxy for 'risk'.

In the USA the concept was rapidly accepted and developed by performance measurers. In the UK, by contrast, the market was slower to accept the usefulness of such risk proxies. The evolution of the debate in both areas is a complex issue and a full chapter is devoted to risk later in the book (Chapter 8).

Growth of peer group data

Building on the early success of their Funds Evaluation Service, A G Becker built up a substantial client base which provided a suitable source for a peer group universe. This was later to evolve into the SEI Corporation with a comprehensive range of universes. Investment consultants, such as Frank Russell, also began to accumulate performance data and to build universe data while, in the international field, InterSec Research built a universe of non-US funds. The Trust Banks themselves also co-operated to form the Trust Universe Comparison Service (TUCS) which is operated by Wilshire Associates.

In the UK the actuarial organisations, which were already servicing pension funds, introduced performance measurement services and quickly saw the benefit of combining resources to provide a wider universe base. Thus Combined Actuarial Performance Services (CAPS) was born to provide performance measurement for pension funds with comparison against both index benchmarks and a universe of other pension funds.

Other organisations, geared to provide fund valuation services to portfolios, also saw the opportunities offered by these developments. Wood, Mackenzie & Co, an Edinburgh based stockbroker, with a department devoted to providing several computer based valuation and analyses services, entered the market in the early seventies and quickly established an important market position. (Later to evolve as The WM Company.)

On both sides of the Atlantic it became apparent that performance measurement with indices as benchmarks was only part of the process. The establishment of a representative and widely based universe of funds under measurement became a prerequisite of a successful service.

The next chapter examines the evolution of market indices and their adoption for performance measurement services and the growth of peer group universes as an alternative benchmark.

The issues

What issues have arisen from the evolution of performance measurement? One source of contention from the fund management end of the spectrum is the argument that the performance measurement companies have been guilty of engineering products and foisting them on to the market. At the basic performance measurement level such a claim can hardly be justified. The evidence of the early discussions in the sixties shows that both the fiduciaries and the ultimate beneficiaries were concerned about the performance of their assets. The providers of the services were clearly responding to a demand which was emerging in the market place.

As often happens the advent of technology, in this case fast computing power, allowed supply and demand to come together. This explosion in information technology meant that the performance of fund managers fell under the spotlight. Such examination would inevitably embarrass some managers just as it re-enforced the pre-eminence of others.

A further contentious issue has been the argument that the short time intervals used for valuation, and hence performance measurement purposes, has placed unwanted pressures on funds to perform over the short term – the accusation of 'short-termism'. This is more difficult to refute but the fault may be with the interpretation of the information rather than in the nature of the data. To carry out many of the functions in performance measurement and analysis, large numbers of observations over short time intervals are necessary, not least to achieve reasonable accuracy. The initial observation of the BAI and the SIA emphasised, however, that interpretation should concentrate on the longer term periods – usually three to five years. One solution may be to make the measurement interval shorter, e.g. monthly, which would provide more data for statistical analysis but would be so short as to be ignored for evaluation purposes.

The pressures towards 'short-termism' are more likely to come from the commercial pressures in the fund management industry than from the performance measurement industry.

The benchmarks

Introduction

From the relatively early years in the life of established stock exchanges the need to monitor the general movements in stock and share prices has been recognised.

Participants in the market, investors and traders alike, followed the movements of individual stock and share prices intently. The speed and efficiency with which this information could be disseminated depended upon the state of information technology. From the carrier pigeon, through the advent of telegraphy and radio transmission to today's advanced international data networks and real time satellite links the demand has been for faster information transmission.

As well as the interest in individual share prices, market participants have also been keen for information on the level and direction of general market movements – what is happening in 'the market'. To do this it is necessary to group together the information on the shares traded on the market in some aggregate or average form. The usual method in the early years was to take a representative sample of shares and group them together to calculate an index.

This chapter examines the evolution of such indices and other benchmarks which have been developed to provide information on asset performance.

Early index development

Some of the longest standing examples of market indices are the Dow-Jones series representing the New York Stock Exchange. The Dow-Jones Industrial Average started in 1884 and was based on the simple average of eleven share prices, subsequently increased to thirty shares. Other Dow-Jones indices were developed: the Utility Average based on 15 utility stocks and the Transportation

Average based on 20 transport stocks, mainly railroad and airline companies. The Dow-Jones Composite Average combined all three.

As a relatively simple price-weighted index based on a limited number of shares it lent itself to easy calculation before the days of electronic calculators and computers. It provided a timely indicator of the general direction and scale of share price changes in the market. The methodology was to add the prices of the constituent shares and divide by a divisor. At its simplest the divisor was the number of shares, but this had to be adjusted to take account of capitalisation changes such as scrip issues.

The drawback to such an index is that high priced shares have an undue influence on the index, taking no account of the total capitalisation of the company nor of the proportional movement in share prices. Thus a $10 rise in the price of a $100 share had the same impact as a $10 rise in the price of a $20 share.

Similarly in the UK the Financial Times Industrial Ordinary Index established widespread acceptance after its launch in 1935 as the key indicator of price movements on the Stock Exchange, London. It was also based on the shares of 30 leading industrial companies but was calculated using a *geometric* average of the share prices, i.e. it *multiplied* the 30 share prices and took the 30th root. As such the index could never represent a 'live' portfolio experience and, indeed, would underestimate the performance of the underlying constituent shares over time. It did, however, overcome the problem exhibited by the arithmetic price average. It also had a major computational disadvantage in that should a constituent share price fall to zero the total index value falls to zero. Thus constituent changes had to be introduced to anticipate such an event.

Providing a benchmark for the performance of live portfolios was never the intention of such indices, however. It was to provide a quick indicator of general price trends on a short-term basis and this they have both done, successfully, to the present day and both are still widely used.

Performance measurement benchmarks

For performance measurement purposes, participants require an index which will reflect the experience of the sum of investors' portfolios of shares in that market. To do this the index must take account of not only the price movements of individual shares but also the total number of such shares in issue, i.e. the market capitalisation of the companies included in the index.

What proportion of the companies quoted should be included depends on various factors. Normally the aim should be to achieve good representation across industries and to encompass at least 60% of the total capitalisation of the market.

The Standard & Poor's indices in the USA were among the first to satisfy these requirements. The main 'S&P 500' Index covered the major stocks on the New York Stock Exchange and has a history back to 1923. It is a capitalisation weighted arithmetic index[1] and continues to serve as a long term market benchmark in the USA.

The 'S&P 500' was restricted to the major companies, however, and covered less than 70% of the value of US traded equities. Frank Russell Company launched a series of broader based indices in the form of the Russell 1000 Index and the Russell 2000 Index covering the top 1000 and next 2000 stocks and accounting for 97% of total market capitalisation: Wilshire Associates also launched the Wilshire 5000 covering companies down to a relatively small capitalisation across all US markets.

In the UK, various indices were developed along similar lines by organisations involved in the financial markets such as Moody's. The Institute of Actuaries and Faculty of Actuaries developed their series of market and sector indices in 1930 following the publication of a paper by C M Douglas[2] but with a restricted valuation frequency and mailing list. It was not until the launch of the Financial Times–Actuaries All Share Index series in 1962 that a comprehensive capitalisation weighted market index became available as a widely accepted benchmark. This resulted from a major update and expansion of the original Actuaries series.

Other markets developed their own local market index, generally, using one or other of the formats described. For example in Tokyo the Nikkei Average, using the Dow formula but covering 225 shares, was launched with a base date of 1949, subsequently rebased to January 1968. The constituents have now been increased to 300 shares.

The Tokyo Stock Exchange catered for participants requiring a capitalisation weighted index by introducing the TSE First Section (for larger companies) and the TSE Second Section (for smaller companies) Indices. These covered some 1200 and over 400 stocks respectively to provide comprehensive coverage of the market with calculations backdated to January 1968.

Thus by the sixties, when performance measurement of portfolios was becoming well established, most markets were able to provide a local market benchmark.

Table 2.1 lists the most commonly used local market equity indices currently available.

---

[1] For a technical description of this as well as the arithmetic price weighted and geometric price indices see Appendix 1.

[2] 'The Statistical Groundwork of Investment Policy', C M Douglas (1930), *Transactions of the Faculty of Actuaries*, 12 173-228.

Table 2.1 Commonly used local market equity indices

North America
USA S & P Composite
   Dow Jones
   Russell 1000
   Russell 2000
   Wilshire 5000
Canada Toronto Composite
   Vancouver SE Index

South America
Argentina General
Brazil Bovespa
Chile IPGA Gen.
Mexico IPC

South Africa
Johannesburg Industrial
   Gold

Far East
Australia All Ord
   Industrial
India BSE Sens.
Indonesia Jakarta SE Index
JF Nusantara Index
Japan Nikkei Dow
   TOPIX
   TSE 2nd Section
Malaysia Kuala Lumpar SE Index
New Zealand 40 Stock Index
Phillipines Manila SE Index
Singapore OCBC Index
   SES Index
   Straits Times
South Korean Composite Index
Taiwan SE Weighted Index
Thailand Set Index

Europe
Austria Credit Aktien Index
Belgium Brussels SE Index
Denmark Copenhagen SE Index
Finland Hex General
France CAC 40

Germany Commerzbank Index
   DAX Index
   FAZ Index
Greece Athens SE General
Ireland Goodbody Total
   JE Davy Index
   SE Index
Italy BCI Index
Netherlands CBS All Share
   CBS Total Return
Norway Oslo SE Index

Portugal BTA Index
Spain Madrid SE Index
Sweden Affarsvarlden Index
Switzerland Verein Industrial
Turkey Istanbul Index

UK
UK FT-SE Actuaries All-Share
   FT-SE 100
   FT-SE 250
   FT-SE Small Cap

Sector and size analysis

As well as providing an overall market index the more comprehensive capitalisation weighted indices such as the S&P, the FT–Actuaries and the TSE First Section (now known as TOPIX) also provide a series of sub-indices. These can be defined by size (e.g. largest capitalisation stocks, mid-size, smallest) or by industry or economic classification groupings. For example the FT–Actuaries All Share Index, now called the FT–SE Actuaries Share Indices following a comprehensive revision at end 1993, provides sub-indices as shown in Table 2.2.

From the table it can be seen that extra information, in addition to the index value, is provided. This is in response to demands from the participants in the market. Dividend yield, earnings yield and price/earnings ratio have been required values for many years and assist in the evaluation and analysis of portfolio performance. The calculation and publication of indices of total return is a relatively recent development. To facilitate the calculation it is necessary to have accurate data on dividend payments and the dates on which shares become quoted 'ex-dividend'. Hence the XD adj. year to date (ytd) column which provides information on the cumulative value of dividends declared and which have gone ex-dividend.

Thus the earlier approximations used for dividends received and the calculation of total returns for the index have become more refined as data availability and computational power have improved. As the computation of portfolio performance has improved in accuracy and frequency so the benchmarks have had to become more refined and accurate.

The series at the top of the table (FT–SE 100, Mid 250, etc) have been published as sub-sets of the FT–Actuaries series. Initially the FT–SE 100 was established in response to demands for an index calculated in real time, (i.e. minute by minute) which would serve as a basis for index futures trading. The FT-SE 250 index followed and at end 1993 administration of the FT–SE series was combined with the FT–A Index to produce the comprehensive FT–SE Actuaries series now available.

The growth of international investment

The indices covered so far have been designed for local markets only. As investors began to invest internationally and create more geographically diversified portfolios so the demand for suitable benchmarks appeared. In the early days international portfolios were either benchmarked against the local index of the investor or against a series of local market indices covering the shares held in the portfolio. The limitations of the latter approach were that the local market indices available would often have different methodologies (e.g. different algorithms for index calculation), different share selection criteria and

Table 2.2 FT–SE Actuaries Share Indices – the UK series

	May 4	Day's chge%	May 3	May 2	May 1	Year ago	Div. yield%	Net cover	P/E ratio	Xd adj. ytd	Total Return
FT-SE 100	3264.3	+0.1	3262.6	3248.2	3220.4	3106.0	4.18	1.97	15.16	54.06	1268.25
FT-SE Mid 250	3560.0	+0.3	3548.7	3542.8	3529.3	3770.6	3.63	1.80	19.07	47.14	1359.80
FT-SE Mid 250 ex Inv Trusts	565.5	+0.3	3554.7	3550.7	3538.6	3787.7	3.78	1.86	17.75	49.42	1360.80
FT-SE-A 350	1619.8	+0.1	1618.0	1611.8	1599.7	1579.7	4.06	1.94	15.89	25.63	1286.73
FT-SE-A 350 Higher Yield	1632.8	+0.1	1631.7	1625.6	1613.9	1570.9	4.99	1.72	14.61	33.19	1070.88
FT-SE-A 350 Lower Yield	1606.7	+0.2	604.2	1597.9	1585.4	1547.9	2.98	2.37	17.69	17.58	1071.42
FT-SE Small Cap	1800.25	+0.5	1790.53	1782.71	1773.71	1941.68	3.36	1.59	23.39	22.50	1425.70
FT-SE Small Cap ex Inv Trusts	1777.76	+0.5	1768.24	1760.96	1751.97	1921.31	3.57	1.65	21.17	23.26	1413.49
FT-SE-A All Share	1600.38	+0.1	1598.05	1591.88	1580.26	1572.45	4.01	1.92	16.29	24.91	1292.51

■ FT–SE Actuaries All-Share

	May 4	Day's chge %	May 3	May 2	May 1	Year ago	Div. yield %	Net cover	P/E ratio	Xd adj. ytd	Total Return
10 MINERAL EXTRACTION (24)	2863.75	+0.3	2854.81	2851.17	2828.58	2681.94	3.60	1.96	17.70	52.95	1179.24
12 Extractive Industries (7)	3731.48	+0.6	3710.66	3724.11	3713.08	3873.64	3.77	1.96	16.88	91.94	1056.64
15 Oil Integrated (3)	2868.05	+0.3	2859.43	2852.00	2827.24	2624.71	3.69	2.05	16.55	50.43	1206.86
16 Oil Exploration & Prod (14)	2099.87	-0.1	2101.11	2104.68	2082.74	1988.30	2.35	0.72	73.59	31.57	1235.43
20 GEN INDUSTRIAL (279)	1913.61	+0.5	1903.77	1893.49	1884.26	2100.46	4.10	1.65	18.44	31.18	1001.18
21 Building & Construction (38)	969.10	+0.2	967.37	969.85	967.64	1324.07	4.10	1.89	16.13	17.71	779.54
22 Building Matls & Merchs (31)	1754.41	+0.4	1747.10	1742.24	1730.96	2056.43	4.22	1.91	15.54	34.53	851.62
23 Chemicals (22)	2320.95	+0.3	2314.57	2316.85	2307.49	2542.03	4.07	1.38	22.18	33.48	1053.35
24 Diversified Industrials (18)	1855.19	+0.5	1845.23	1837.59	1831.72	2098.53	5.14	1.46	16.64	40.72	982.76
25 Electronic & Elec Equip (37)	2008.81	+1.2	1984.11	1965.17	1959.22	2045.49	3.63	1.92	17.88	14.64	1000.14
26 Engineering (72)	1908.27	+0.3	1902.32	1881.67	1864.51	1968.90	3.25	1.87	20.55	23.87	1114.86
27 Engineering, Vehicles (13)	2259.60	-0.3	2265.31	2231.22	2223.72	2449.44	4.05	0.49	63.03	47.72	1130.79
28 Paper, Pckg & Printing (27)	2912.97	+0.1	2883.45	2872.88	2863.42	2941.07	3.28	2.31	16.48	38.72	1169.63
29 Textiles & Apparel (21)	1612.87	+0.6	1603.39	1600.71	1592.66	1811.88	4.38	1.63	17.56	26.92	939.84
30 CONSUMER GOODS (94)	3074.57	?	3074.11	3055.29	3042.87	2739.37	4.23	1.71	17.28	57.81	1090.01
31 Breweries (18)	2340.74	+0.4	2332.02	2296.89	2285.34	2296.24	4.14	2.03	14.88	12.45	1072.63
32 Spirits, Wines & Ciders (10)	2771.82	-0.3	2780.43	2759.66	2749.91	2976.30	4.19	1.83	16.32	54.52	956.31
33 Food Producers (24)	2460.35	+0.2	2455.04	2446.11	2436.74	2353.94	4.13	1.95	15.49	53.07	1070.34
34 Household Goods (10)	2558.95	-0.2	2563.06	2512.04	2495.96	2730.11	3.60	0.86	40.19	50.32	946.03
36 Health Care (18)	1746.06	+0.5	1737.10	1719.97	1713.08	1719.72	2.97	0.97	43.26	23.68	1034.16
37 Pharmaceuticals (12)	3828.62	+0.1	3825.46	3800.83	3788.68	2784.75	4.06	1.57	19.65	61.12	1249.29
38 Tobacco (2)	4004.02	-0.5	4023.61	4043.46	4016.28	3745.73	5.66	1.63	13.53	131.29	947.66
40 SERVICES (229)	1989.66	+0.2	1985.85	1979.66	1966.13	2050.55	3.29	2.09	18.16	23.35	998.33
41 Distributors (32)	2457.66	+0.7	2440.45	2434.71	2447.66	3051.60	3.89	1.95	16.50	44.19	875.26
42 Leisure & Hotels (29)	2252.96	+0.4	2245.05	2254.13	2215.35	2235.94	3.41	1.58	23.14	35.81	1136.35
43 Media (43)	2948.16	-0.1	2951.35	2898.91	2865.07	3086.88	2.66	2.28	20.68	48.91	1044.57
44 Retailers, Food (16)	1902.48	-0.6	1913.79	1912.69	1924.12	1643.73	3.55	2.47	14.25	17.14	1158.76
45 Retailers, General (44)	1675.65	+0.3	1670.87	1670.35	1653.53	1762.30	3.28	2.12	17.94	11.49	918.65
48 Support Services (37)	1558.76	+0.6	1548.97	1553.66	1546.59	1669.39	2.75	2.42	18.81	13.59	963.48
49 Transport (21)	2242.47	+0.8	2224.51	2222.64	2214.32	2500.21	3.83	1.89	17.23	29.32	897.59
51 Other Services & Business (7)	1243.33	?	1243.32	1240.47	1232.95	1217.43	3.63	1.21	28.35	10.90	1088.68
60 UTILITIES (37)	2335.87	-0.2	2339.55	2345.47	2319.76	2214.86	4.66	1.93	13.92	6.85	920.35
62 Electricity (17)	2217.72	+0.1	2214.63	2230.01	2225.01	2101.27	4.61	2.67	10.17	19.89	949.08
64 Gas Distribution (2)	2025.80	-0.9	2045.00	2048.44	2016.82	1881.94	5.91	0.65	32.39	0.00	951.50
66 Telecommunications (5)	2029.32	-0.1	2031.17	2033.15	1994.33	1976.30	4.03	1.68	18.46	0.13	880.77
68 Water (13)	1835.30	-0.1	1837.86	1836.64	1840.94	1665.13	5.45	2.73	8.39	4.62	935.84
69 NON-FINANCIALS (663)	1727.74	+0.2	1724.52	1718.86	1707.71	1707.83	3.96	1.84	17.14	24.09	1252.21
70 FINANCIALS (117)	2301.44	+0.1	2304.29	2289.66	2263.46	2162.58	4.60	2.34	11.62	58.71	944.03
71 Banks, Retail (9)	3073.64	-0.4	3087.35	3067.72	3030.28	2706.05	4.47	2.95	9.46	86.03	954.00
72 Banks, Merchant (8)	3286.68	+0.3	3277.93	3298.31	3219.90	2886.12	3.52	2.54	13.95	31.67	1008.58
73 Insurance (26)	1285.23	-0.3	1289.63	1270.90	1254.46	1306.79	5.52	1.67	13.53	42.72	920.75
74 Life Assurance (6)	2559.10	+0.9	2537.03	2520.96	2501.57	2377.47	5.31	1.33	17.72	91.02	1026.83
77 Other Financial (22)	1986.47	-0.1	1988.27	1985.67	1976.50	1887.28	3.86	2.32	13.94	25.59	1087.86
79 Property (46)	1367.32	+0.7	1357.42	1351.27	1341.72	1626.43	4.40	1.19	23.89	12.85	800.87
80 INVESTMENT TRUSTS (113)	2729.39	+0.4	2717.72	2702.35	2683.92	2829.08	2.33	1.03	51.92	20.96	929.65
89 FT-SE-A ALL-SHARE (913)	1600.38	-0.1	1598.05	1591.88	1580.26	1572.45	4.01	1.92	16.29	24.91	1292.51
FT-SE-A Fledgling	982.28	+0.6	976.77	974.25	971.46	-	3.07	1.12	36.21	10.65	993.15
FT-SE-A Fledgling ex Inv Trusts	976.07	+0.5	971.23	968.97	966.16	-	3.25	1.15	33.30	11.16	987.40

■ Hourly movements

	Open	9.00	10.00	11.00	12.00	13.00	14.00	15.00	16.10	High/Day	Low/Day
FT-SE 100	3283.5	3282.9	3282.9	3270.9	3273.8	3275.6	3278.4	3271.7	3263.9	3288.2	3260.6
FT-SE Mid 250	3558.7	3558.2	3561.0	3559.8	3560.0	3559.3	3560.3	3560.4	3559.8	3561.3	3557.0
FT-SE-A 350	1627.1	1626.8	1628.7	1622.3	1623.4	1624.1	1625.3	1622.7	1619.6	1629.0	1618.1

Time of FT-SE100 Day's high: 9.49am Day's low: 3.16pm FT-SE 100 1995 High: 226.2(26/4) Low: 2954.2(23/1)

■ FT–SE Actuaries 350 Industry baskets

	Open	9.00	10.00	11.00	12.00	13.00	14.00	15.00	16.10	Close	Previous	Change
Bldg & Cnstrcn	955.1	954.1	953.6	952.4	952.4	951.9	952.5	952.5	952.5	952.4	952.5	-0.1
Pharmaceuticls	3817.1	3815.0	3812.6	3799.8	3802.7	3814.8	3816.1	3804.7	3795.7	3794.6	3791.5	+3.1
Water	1830.3	1830.7	1828.9	1829.8	1831.8	1831.5	1832.0	1829.7	1828.7	1828.7	1831.2	-2.5
Banks, Retail	3139.1	3140.2	3148.5	3128.4	3131.4	3131.2	3130.8	3120.2	3111.1	3112.9	3126.7	-13.8

16

different timing and sourcing of basic price data. Moreover they could not be combined satisfactorily into a global index.

Capital Group Inc (a California based investment manager) recognised the limitations and undertook the considerable task, in the sixties, of creating a world index which would comprise a series of country sub-indices covering the major investment markets and constructed on a consistent basis. Working from a base in Geneva, Switzerland, their subsidiary, Capital International SA, launched the Capital International World Index (CIWI) in 1970. Apart from the global and national market indices the series also included geographic regional indices and 38 international industry indices. The series rapidly became established as a benchmark for international portfolios and was the only such index series until 1987.

The acquisition of the rights to the Capital International Indices by Morgan Stanley (a US brokerage and finance house) in 1986 appeared to stimulate the creation of rival indices involving other major brokerage and finance houses:

- The Financial Times–Actuaries World Index (created by a joint venture between the FT, the Actuaries, Goldman Sachs and Wood, Mackenzie);[3]

- The Salomon Russell World Index (created by a joint venture between Salomon Brothers and Frank Russell who were already responsible for a series of wide-coverage indices in the USA);

- The Euromoney First Boston World Index (created by a joint venture between the Euromoney publication company and First Boston).

All these series were capitalisation weighted indices with comprehensive coverage of the major markets.

For example the Capital International series, now Morgan Stanley Capital International (MSCI) covers around 1500 companies in 22 countries representing around 60% of the total capitalisation of the combined markets. The FT–Actuaries World Index, now designated the FT/S&P Actuaries World Indices (FT/S&P–AWI), covers over 2200 companies in 26 countries and aims to represent around 75% of each country's total market capitalisation. Both series also produce international industry indices and, in addition the FT/S&P-AWI series extends the industry classification down to the country level.

The indices are calculated in local currencies and in several of the major currencies (US dollar, sterling, Deutschmark, yen). Thus although not

---

[3] In 1995 Wood, Mackenzie, by then part of NatWest Securities ceased direct involvement in production of the indices (assumed by the FT) and Standard & Poor became involved in the US. The series is now designated the FT/S&P Actuaries World Indices. (FT/S&P AW1)

Table 2.3 FT/S&P Actuaries World Index structure – constituent distribution at 31/03/95

	USA	BRAZ	CAN	MEX	AUST	BELG	DEN	FIN	FR	GER	IRE	ITA	NETH	NOR	SPA	SWED	SWIT	UK	AUSL	HK	JPN	MAL	NZ	SING	THAI	SA	TOTAL
Finance/Insurance	78	4	24	4	6	17	7	5	30	14	4	30	3	4	12	9	13	52	19	25	61	30	2	16	26	12	507
Banks-Commercial/Oth	30	3	9	1	6	7	4	3	5	6	2	7	1	2	8	3	4	10	7	2	28	5		5	10	3	171
Financial/Inst/Serv	15		4	1		2			11	1	1	4						18	2	2	17	6	2	1	10	1	97
Ins-Life/Agent/Brker	12	1								1		1						6								3	24
Ins-Mult/Prop/Caslty	14	2	2		2	4	2	2	3	7		13	2	2	1	1	8	5	2		11						79
Real Estate Ex Reit	1		2						5							1		9	8	17	5	13		8	6	5	77
Divers Holding Cos	6	1	6	2		4	1		6			6			1	4	1	4		4		6		2			69
Energy	26	2	15		1		2		3			1	1	4	2		1	4	6	4	10	2	1	1	1	2	82
Oil	20	2	11		1		2		2				1	4	2		1	4	4	4	8	2		1		1	64
Other Energy	6		4		2				1			1							2		2		1		1	1	18
Utilities	68	6	9	2	2	6	2		2	4		5	1		8	2	1	14	1	4	14	2	1	1	2	1	157
Utilities	68	6	9	2	2	6	2		2	4		5	1		8	2	1	14	1	4	14	2	1	1	2	1	157
Transport/Storage	17		4		1		5		1	1			1	11	2		1	6	3	5	27	3	1	3	1	1	93
Transport/Storage	17		4		1		5		1	1			1	11	2		1	6	3	5	27	3	1	3	1	1	93
Consumer Good/Ser	161	3	22	8	4	3	13	6	41	15	8	9	7	6	5	11	16	64	21	19	156	28	6	14	4	11	661
Automobiles	3				1				2	5		3				2					10	4	2				33
H. Hold durab/Apiance	5								3		1					1	2		1	1	10	2	1				29
Divers Cons Gds/Ser	5			1	3		1		1		3						2		3	2							21
Textile/Wearing Appl	6		1						2			1				1		1		1	13						29
Beverage/Tobacco Man	9	1	6	1	3		2		3			1	1		2			11	2		9	2	1	2		3	58
Health/Personal Care	30				1		2		6	2				2		5	4	7	1	22							81

																											Total
Food/Grocery Prods	17		1	1		3	4	5		3	3	2		3			1	10	4		26	11	1	1	1	6	105
Entertain/Leis/Toys	14		3			4		4				1		2				6	1	6	22	6		4	2		67
Media	23		5	1			1	4		1	1	2		1				6	5	2	5	1	2	2	2		64
Bus Serv/Comps.Ware	12				4		2			1						1		6			2	1					26
Retail Trade	30	2	6	4	3	1	2	9	5		1	1		1		4	3	16	2	5	22	1	1	1		2	117
Wholesale Trade	7							1	1									3	2	1	15	1	1	1	1		32
Capital Goods	**97**	**1**	**8**		**2**	**3**	**3**	**12**	**1**	**7**	**3**	**4**	**1**			**13**	**10**	**26**	**8**	**2**	**108**	**6**	**1**	**8**	**3**	**3**	**340**
Aerospace Defence	14						1									1	1	3		1							20
Comps/Comms/Ofce Eqp	19		3			1		2		3						2					16			2		2	47
Electrical Equipment	8		1		1		1	3			1	1				4	4	1		1	12						38
Electronics/Instrumt	15		2			1	2	1	1									6			23	2	2			2	55
Machinery/Eng Serv	14				2	1	1	2		2	1					7	5	7	2		23	1	1	1			74
Auto Components	12		1					3	1	2								3			21	2					45
Divers Indust Manf	13	1	1				1	1	1		1		1					6	5		4	2	1		1		39
Heavy Eng/Shipbuild	2						1					4							1	1	9	1	5				22
Basic Industries	**64**	**12**	**21**	**4**	**11**	**7**	**3**	**12**	**3**	**6**	**6**	**4**	**8**	**13**	**13**	**6**	**37**	**25**	**4**	**108**	**26**	**4**	**2**	**9**	**30**		**443**
Construct/Build Mats	5	2	1	3	7	1	3	6	4	4	4	1	5	3	3	1	21	4		41	14	1	1	8	2		139
Chemicals	25	1	1		2	4		2	1	1		2	1	2	2	2	7	1	1	31	3	1		1	1		93
Mining-Metal/Mineral	9	6	8			2	2	2				1	1	2	2		2	10		20	5		1		4		82
Precious-Metals/Mins	5		6														1	9		1					21		44
Forestry/Paper Prods	16	3	4	1	2		6	1	2		1	2		6		1	3	1		7	2	3	1	2	2		65
Fabr Metal Prods	4		1														3			8	2						20
Market	**511**	**28**	**103**	**18**	**27**	**35**	**33**	**24**	**101**	**59**	**16**	**58**	**19**	**33**	**38**	**48**	**47**	**203**	**83**	**55**	**484**	**97**	**14**	**44**	**46**	**59**	**2283**

Source: NatWest Securities Ltd.

specifically published, a comprehensive exchange rate series can also be derived from the data.

Table 2.3 shows the matrix of countries and industries covered by the FT/S&P–AWI series.

Variations between these index series are relatively modest and, apart from different country or industry groupings, tend to be limited to the selection criteria for inclusion in the index. Some of the indices exclude shares unavailable to non-resident investors, for example. Others calculate capitalisations excluding cross holdings or blocked holdings. The source and timing for the basic data collection may also vary between indices, particularly where they are managed from different time zones. (For more discussion on the complexities of data collection see Chapter 6.)

Although the availability of these international indices satisfied the demands for a basic global benchmark the expansion of international investment led to further developments. As investors explored the less developed markets and the markets, in their turn, developed to allow or encourage foreign participants, the need for further index series became apparent. Thus in 1993 MSCI launched their Emerging Market Indices applying the methodology of the basic MSCI series to a further 14 emerging markets encompassing 540 companies. These were:– Argentina, Brazil, Chile, Greece, Indonesia, Jordan, Korea, Malaysia, Mexico, Portugal, Philippines, Taiwan, Thailand and Turkey. In addition, six regional indices were created and the series can be combined with the basic MSCI Indices to create an all country index.

Other specialised emerging market indices had also been launched by other brokerage and finance houses. Baring Securities launched their Emerging Markets Index in October 1992, now covering 13 countries (the MSCI list excluding Jordan) with around 240 companies selected on capitalisation and availability criteria. James Capel introduced their 'Dragon 300 Index' in July 1992 covering 300 companies in eight Pacific Region markets:– Hong Kong, Indonesia, Korea, Malaysia, Philippines, Singapore, Taiwan and Thailand.

Benchmark indices were therefore emerging in response to growing investment diversification.

Customised benchmark indices

In addition to the series of standard indices which have emerged, the complexities of modern portfolio management have led to demands for specialist customised indices. Some investment funds have specific constraints built into their investment mandate. For example during the years of apartheid in South Africa many funds, particularly public service funds in the USA, were prohibited from investing in companies with South African interests. The standard indices were, therefore, unsuitable as a performance benchmark and customised benchmarks which excluded South African connected companies from the indices were created by organisations such as Morgan Stanley.

Similarly funds with ethical constraints (no alcohol or tobacco for example) or environmental constraints (no 'non-green' companies) would require specifically customised benchmark indices for performance measurement purposes.

With most of the world's equity markets now monitored by data collection organisations, and with high powered transmission and computation facilities available, the growth of specialised benchmark indices is likely to continue. Moreover those markets not yet able to provide the level of information necessary to create dividend, earnings and total return data comparable to the sample shown previously for the FT–SE–A series in the UK will be encouraged to move towards these standards.

Bond market and other indices

The indices discussed so far have been exclusively based on equities and provide index benchmarks for equity portfolios only. Their development has been paralleled by the provision of indices for bond portfolios. Investors in bonds have slightly different requirements when considering performance measurement than have equity investors. In many more cases the portfolios are acting under specific constraints, usually related to the duration of the portfolio (to match the duration of the liabilities for example) and to risk (in this context usually default risk).

In the early years it was often unnecessary to compile an index in order to establish a suitable benchmark. In many situations a single 'benchmark' bond would be sufficient. For example the UK Government 2½% Consols would have served as a benchmark for irredeemable gilt-edged stocks and was used alongside the early Actuaries equity series in the UK for that purpose. Similarly a defined US Treasury bond (say the 30 year bond) would serve as the benchmark for minimal risk bonds of a similar duration.

Table 2.4 shows a typical list of benchmark bonds for the major government bond markets. A drawback of using benchmark bonds for performance measurement, however, is that the benchmark inevitably changes with time (as comparison of Table 2.4 with a current equivalent table will illustrate).

Provided the bonds were deemed to have similar risk, which would be defined by established bond rating services such as Moody's and Standard & Poor's, then the key variables between bonds were the coupon and redemption date. Such variables are critical, however, and even small differences can affect the expected performance of the bond, making it unique.

Funds habitually hold a cross section of bonds in their fixed interest portfolios and the demand for benchmark indices saw the establishment of

21

Table 2.4 Benchmark government bonds (as at February 1994)

		Coupon	Red Date
Australia		9.500	08/04
Belgium		7.250	04/04
Canada		7.500	12/03
Denmark		7.000	12/04
France	BTAN	8.000	05/98
	OAT	5.500	04/04
Germany		6.000	09./03
Italy		8.500	01/04
Japan	No 119	4.800	06/99
	No 157	4.500	06/03
Netherlands		5.750	01/04
Spain		10.500	10/03
UK Gilts		9.750	01/98
		6.750	11/04
		9.000	10/08
US Treasury		5.750	08/03
		6.250	08/23
ECU (French Govt)		6.000	04/04

several varieties in the major markets. In the UK, the FT–Fixed Interest Indices became established as benchmarks following their launch in the 1920s. In the USA, Dow-Jones established their Home Bonds Index to compliment their equity index series.

These indices, although still published, failed to provide the requirements for more detailed benchmarks for more complex portfolios. In the UK most of these requirements were satisfied by the creation of the FT–Actuaries Fixed Interest Indices. This series divided the government bond market by redemption date or maturity and by coupon yield.

Table 2.5 shows the structure of the series as currently presented. In addition to the UK Government issues, an index of non-government Debentures and Loan Stocks was also produced. (The Debentures and Loan Stocks was discontinued at the end of 1994 as low trading volume made pricing more difficult and more business switched to the Eurocurrency markets.) This series of indices satisfied most of the requirements for fixed interest portfolios in the UK, particularly since the government securities market was by far the dominant

Table 2.5 FT–Actuaries fixed interest indices

Price Indices UK Gilts	Tue May 4	Day's change %	Mon May 3	Accrued interest	xd adj ytd		....Low coupon yield----			...Medium coupon yield---			....High coupon yield.....		
							May 4	May 3	Yr ago	May 4	May 3	Yr ago	May 4	May 3	Yr ago
1 Up to 5 years (23)	119.52	+0.21	119.26	1.38	4.27	5 yrs	8.21	8.29	7.83	8.27	8.35	8.04	8.41	8.49	8.15
2 5-15 years to (21)	141.22	+0.48	141.05	1.02	5.44	15 yrs	8.24	8.30	8.16	8.31	8.38	8.25	8.52	8.58	8.55
3 Over 15 years (9)	160.02	+0.59	159.07	2.24	4.74	20 yrs	8.23	8.29	8.16	8.31	8.38	8.25	8.44	8.51	8.42
4 Irredeemables (6)	180.33	+0.68	179.12	0.13	6.12	Irre.+	8.30	8.36	8.21						
5 All Stocks (59)	138.17	+0.41	137.84	1.36	4.94										

Index-Linked	Tue May 4	Day's change %	Mon May 3	Accrued interest	xd adj ytd		Inflation 5%			Inflation 10%		
							May 4	May 3	Yr. ago	May 4	May 3	Yr ago
6 Up to 5 years (2)	192.39	-0.07	192.52	0.45	2.57	Up to 5 yrs	3.35	3.29	3.51	1.88	1.83	2.57
7 Over 5 years (11)	180.64	+0.40	179.92	0.85	1.73	Over 5 yrs	3.71	3.74	3.58	3.52	3.55	3.40
8 All Stocks (13)	180.96	+0.35	180.33	0.81	1.81							

Average gross redemption yields are shown above. Coupon Bands: Low: 0%-7¾%; Medium: 8%-10¾%; High: 11% and over. + Flat Yield. ytd Year to date.

sector. The Government Securities Index had its base in 1926 while the Fixed Interest Index (covering corporate and other debentures and loan stocks) started in 1928.

In the USA, although the dominance of US Treasury issues was also a feature of the market, there was a much wider market in corporate, agency and mortgage issues. The demand for a more comprehensive series of bond indices was met by the leading brokerage/dealing houses in the market such as Merrill Lynch. Other major bond market traders such as Salomon Brothers, J P Morgan and Lehman Brothers also produced their own proprietary index series. The Merrill Lynch series is a good example of the comprehensive indices published by such organisations.

The US domestic market was comprehensively covered in their Domestic Taxable Bond Indices which were sub-divided into a Domestic Master Series and a High Yield Master Series. The former covers US Treasury Issues, Agency issues, Corporate issues of investment grade (i.e. BBB/Baa or better under the S&P/Moody's ratings) and Mortgages. The latter covered the lower end corporate issues (i.e. ratings of less than investment grade but not in default). Each area is further sub-divided by maturity and, within the corporate bond sector, by investment grade and industry. In all over 200 separate indices!

This provides considerable flexibility for market participants who can not only make use of the general indices as performance benchmarks but can also create customised indices by combining suitable sub-indices to reflect their operating portfolios. As with the evolution of equity indices the essential feature was to ensure that the index was a reasonable reflection of investable opportunity. Securities were therefore screened for marketability and compatibility with typical investment practice.

International bond indices

Also in parallel with equities the demand for international benchmarks mirrored the expansion of international bond investment. In this area the established US brokerage houses led the field by adding foreign coverage to their already comprehensive domestic index series. In the 1970s the main interest of US investors centred on the exploding growth in the Eurobond market and Merrill Lynch incorporated a series of Eurodollar indices within their overall series. This covered supranational, sovereign, US Corporate, Japanese, Canadian and 'All Others' in a series of sub-indices split by maturity.

In Europe the long experience in international bond investment of the Swiss provided an obvious launching pad for the Lombard Odier & Cie Bond Indices. As interest expanded investors turned their attention to the local currency issues of foreign governments and international bodies although the government issues dominate most markets and their, generally, higher investment grade makes them the preferred medium for most international investors.

Consequently the more recent developments in international indices have concentrated on government bonds with strict screening on investability and liquidity. Salomon Brothers launched their New Salomon Brothers World Government Bond Index in 1986 (base 31 December 1984) as the first stage in a redesign of their existing World Bond Index which also covered Eurobonds. The matrix of that index at 1 October 1986 is shown in Table 2.6. The series of indices were published monthly, originally. (A current version of this index would be more comprehensive in coverage.)

Demand from investors and the competition in the market for proprietary indices led to the introduction of indices with more frequent and timely publication. In 1990 J P Morgan Securities introduced their Government Bond Index with daily calculation and publication, with a base date 31 December 1987 but with daily data back to 31 December 1985. Table 2.7 shows the statistical profile of the J P Morgan GBI as at 1 November 1990.

Such indices were designed to meet the demand for benchmarks not only for normal international bond portfolios but also for the growing trend towards indexed funds. The ability to replicate the index with a 'live' portfolio was therefore critical and considerations of liquidity and frequency of index adjustment were high on the agenda.

Lehman Brothers also introduced daily calculation when launching their Global Government Bond Index covering 19 countries with a sub-set – the Majors Index – covering 13 countries. Currently these organisations all value daily. Table 2.8 summarises the characteristics of the major index series currently widely used for performance measurement as at 31 December 1992.

Apart from the basic indices calculated in the major currencies most of these international bond index series calculate indices on the assumption that currency exposure is hedged back into the base currency – 'hedged indices'. All these bond indices are produced by the brokerage/finance houses and their structure and calculation algorithms can differ as shown in Table 2.8. Indices are constantly refined and developed and the data shown in the table may change.

In Europe there was a concern that a bond index series should be available for the major markets with a common methodology and in the 1980s the EFFAS and European Bond Commission (EFFAS–EBC) began development of such a series. The aim was to produce a series which was transparent as to its method of construction and stock selection and which would enable fair comparison between national markets. With the support of Bloomberg LP and the International Securities Market Association (ISMA) the Bloomberg/EFFAS indices were launched in the early 1990s. A practical guide to this series and a

Table 2.6 Summary profile of the Salomon Brothers World Government Bond Index, 1 October 1986

	US	Japan	UK	West Germany	France	Canada	Netherlands	Australia	Switzerland	World Govt Bond Index
No of Issues	159	96	91	124	41	118	107	100	45	881
Principal Amount	$841.0	$473.3	$153.1	$78.1	$57.3	$58.4	$52.0	$21.1	$7.4	$1,741.7
Market Value	$971.8	$516.8	$153.6	$87.1	$71.3	$66.1	$59.5	$20.1	$7.7	$1,954.0
Market Weight	49.8%	26.4%	7.9%	4.5%	3.6%	3.4%	3.0%	1.0%	0.4%	100.0%
Average Coupon	10.02%	6.99%	10.62%	7.62%	11.34%	11.27%	8.67%	12.19%	4.91%	9.19%
AverageMaturity (Yrs)	8.28	4.92	11.70	6.52	7.91	9.69	5.54	6.45	7.09	7.51
Yield to Maturity	7.20%	5.10%	10.90%	5.68%	7.54%	9.33%	5.98%	14.48%	4.50%	6.98%
Nominal Duration (Yrs)	4.86	4.08	5.62	5.04	5.33	5.59	4.35	3.98	5.93	4.74

Table 2.7 Profile of the J P Morgan Government Bond Index, 1 November 1990

		Australia	Belgium	Canada	France	Germany	Italy	Japan	Netherlands	Spain	United Kingdom	United States	Global
		CGSs	BGBs	Canadas	OATs BTANs EEs	Bund, Bahn Post, Unilies Bobls, Kassen	BTPs CTOs	JGBs	DSLs Obligaciones	Bonos	Gilts	Treasuries	
Number of issues	Traded	16	13	43	31	62	17	38	40	5	33	147	445
	Active	12	7	30	19	36	6	8	18	4	24	21	185
	Bench	8	1	6	5	2	3	1	1	1	8	7	43
Par Value (US$ bil)	Eligible	20	106	109	188	241	187	566	108	34	184	1331	3074
	Traded	16	49	74	136	172	95	325	92	26	127	1150	2261
	Active	14	24	53	107	116	39	107	48	20	103	217	848
	Bench	10	2	11	32	11	26	14	6	6	38	78	233
Market Weight (%)	Eligible	0.6	3.4	3.5	5.9	7.5	6.1	16.8	3.4	0.8	5.8	46.1	100
	Traded	0.7	2.1	3.2	5.7	7.1	4.1	13.1	3.9	1.1	5.4	53.6	100
	Active	1.7	2.8	6.4	12.2	13.4	4.5	11.8	5.6	2.5	12.1	27.1	100
	Bench	4.7	0.7	4.8	11.8	4.8	10.8	5.5	2.6	2.8	16.1	35.5	100
Coverage Ratio[a]		81	46	68	72	71	50	58	85	76	69	86	74
Avge Coupon (% pa)	Traded	12.6	9.0	10.2	8.9	7.1	12.5	5.4	7.6	13.0	10.6	9.4	8.7
	Active	12.6	9.1	10.1	8.9	7.4	12.5	5.5	7.8	13.1	10.6	8.6	8.5
	Bench	12.5	10.0	10.6	8.4	8.9	12.5	4.8	9.0	13.8	10.2	8.6	9.2
Avg Maturity (years)	Traded	5.4	5.5	8.2	7.2	6.2	3.7	6.9	6.4	2.3	8.5	7.6	7.1
	Active	5.8	6.4	8.3	8.2	6.8	4.7	7.9	8.5	2.5	8.6	7.2	7.4
	Bench	6.1	9.8	11.4	11.8	7.3	5.0	8.6	9.5	2.6	8.6	8.2	8.3
Yield[b] (%)	Traded	13.1	10.0	11.0	10.2	9.0	13.7	7.3	9.1	14.9	11.4	8.4	8.9
	Active	13.1	10.0	10.9	10.2	9.0	13.9	7.3	9.1	14.8	11.4	8.3	9.4
	Bench	13.1	10.1	10.9	10.3	9.0	14.2	7.2	9.1	14.7	11.3	8.3	9.9
Duration (years)	Traded	3.6	4.3	4.7	4.6	4.7	2.8	5.5	4.8	1.9	5.1	4.4	4.5
	Active	3.9	4.9	4.7	5.1	5.2	3.4	6.2	6.1	2.1	5.1	4.3	4.9
	Bench	3.9	6.5	5.3	6.4	5.5	3.5	6.8	6.5	2.2	5.0	4.6	4.9
Convexity (%)	Traded	18.9	22.4	37.2	33.1	29.0	10.4	38.8	31.0	4.7	39.4	39.1	35.6
	Active	20.7	28.1	37.7	38.7	33.5	14.2	45.1	44.8	5.4	39.3	36.0	35.9
	Bench	22.1	49.7	52.4	59.4	37.0	15.8	53.4	50.4	5.9	40.2	42.3	40.2
JPM Location		Sydney	Brussels	Toronto	Paris	Frankfurt	Milan	Tokyo	London	Madrid	London	New York	

a. Coverage ratio is defined as the market value of the traded index divided by the total market size (eligible universe).

b. Yields: annual for Belgium, France, Germany, Italy and Spain; annual equivalent life for the Netherlands; semi-annual otherwise.

Table 2.8 Characteristics of the Major Bond Index Series

Characteristics	J.P. Morgan	Lehman Brothers	Merrill Lynch	Salomon Brothers	Lombard Odier
History from	31/12/85 Daily	1/1/87 Most Countries	31/12/85 Monthly 31/5/90 Daily	31/12/84 Monthly March 1992 Daily	31/12/82 Most Countries
Frequency of Calculation	Daily	Daily	Daily 15:00 EST	Daily	Daily
Issue Eligibility	Liquidity constraints applied Maturity > 1 Year	Maturity > 1 Year Par outstanding rule varies according to country	Public Issues Maturity > 1 Year Par outstanding of $25m for which current prices can be obtained	Maturity > 1 Year Par outstanding rule varies according to country	Maturity > 1 year Minimum SFR 100min or Equivalent
Pricing Source	Local market Closing Prices	Lehman trading desks + affiliated market makers. Prices taken at close of futures markets if available otherwise at close of cash market	Merrill Lynch Trading desks supplemented by other sources as required	Salomon Brothers in major markets, "significant market makers" in others	Several including "major market maker"
X-Rate Source *	17:00 London WM/Reuters Closing Spot Rates	16:00 London WM/Reuters	15:00 EST WM/Reuters	12:30 New York WM/Reuters etc	WM Reuters

*   Since 1994 the index providers have standardised on the WM/Reuters Closing Spot Rates.

Construction Method	Weighted by Market Capitalisation	Market Capitalisation except Japan where only top 40 bonds are used in Capitalisation	Weighted by Market Capitalisation	Weighted by Market Capitalisation	Weighted by Market Capitals. Buy Real CDP for European Bond Index
Treatment of Coupon Flows	Immediate reinvestment of coupons into constituent series	Re-invested monthly	Daily reinvestment of coupons into the constituent series	Reinvestment of intra-month payments into a short term rate until the end of the month	Cumulative and Non-cumulative indices are calculated
Constituent Changes	Once a month for start of each month	Once a month for start each month	Changes are reflected in the index the day after they happen	Once a month for start of each month	Quarterly rebalancing
New Issues	Issues are included from the first business day of the following month	Bonds are added when they are issued, but contribute to returns from the next month	New Issues enter the index on the first business day following settlement	Issues are included from the first business day of the following month	N/A
Number of Bonds in Global Index	424	665	657	807	240
Total Capitalisation of Index (US$ Bn)	3,053	3,602	3,812	4,149	N/A
Maturity Sectors (Years)	1-3, 3-5, 5-7, 10, 10+ or others as requested	1-3, 3-5, 5-7, 10, 10+ or others as requested	1-3, 3-5, 5-7, 10+	1-3, 3-5, 3-7, 4-7, 7-10, 10+ or others as requested	1-3, 3-5, 5-7, 7-10, 10-15, 15-20, 20+

useful indication of the complexities of bond index construction is provided in *Constructing and Calculating Bond Indices.*[4]

Other assets

As funds diversified their investments across asset classes so the demand for suitable benchmarks evolved. Apart from equities and bonds the most commonly held assets are cash (on deposit or in very short-term instruments such as Treasury Bills) and property or real estate.

For cash investment the benchmarks are specific officially quoted rates, for example, in the UK the LIBOR rate for the specified period (7 days or 1 month). In the USA the Treasury Bill rate for 1 to 3 months might be used or the Prime rate for shorter term deposits. Each country usually has an official interest rate market from which a suitable benchmark rate can be chosen.

For property the problem is more complex and it is arguable whether it is ever possible to create a suitable index for the property market. The main difficulties lie in the fact that each property or piece of real estate is unique and that trading, and therefore the establishment of a market price, is infrequent. Nevertheless, by monitoring a wide range of properties and the transactions which take place, combined with the regular valuations which occur, indices of property prices and investment returns have been created. Evaluation Associates in the USA and Investment Property Databank (IPD) in the UK are examples of such developments.

Other assets, such as commodities, are also held by some funds. Gold is the most common example but in such instances the management of the asset cannot add to the basic return from the asset class. Only by trading the asset would the fund manager add (or detract) value from the underlying change in the commodity price. In these cases the benchmark is usually the suitable trading market price, for example, the London Bullion Market for gold prices, the New York or Chicago commodity exchanges for oil prices and soya bean prices respectively.

Fund benchmarks

The need for such wide-ranging benchmarks arises from the diversity of assets held by investment funds. In the case of assets such as equities or bonds, part of the purpose is to judge the management performance within that asset class against the chosen benchmark. At the overall fund level, however, a significant part of management performance derives from the proportions in which the

---

[4] *Constructing and Calculating Bond Indices*, Patrick J Brown, Probus Publishing, 1994.

Table 2.9 Multiple markets index asset class allocations

Assets	% Total Capitalisation	% in MMI
US Domestic Large Capitalisation Equities	11.9	30
Smaller Capitalisation	2.5	15
International Equities	13.1	10
Venture Capital	0.1	5
US Domestic Bonds	20.0	15
International Dollar Bonds	2.1	4
Non Dollar Bonds	22.3	6
Real Estate	14.0	15
Cash Equivalents	9.0	0
	100.0	100

assets are held within the fund and the changes made to those proportions over time. Setting suitable benchmarks for the overall multi-asset fund therefore presents different problems.

One solution is to establish a multi-markets index. This approach takes the individual asset benchmarks or indices and groups them together into a multiple index. The proportions allocated to each index can either be capitalisation weighted or some other defined proportions. This is simply an extension of the approach used for international equity indices. For example, some international investors prefer to create their international equity benchmark by weighting the series of national indices by GDP values or international trade values rather than by capitalisation.

In the USA the Salomon Bond Indices are combined with the Russell Equity Indices to create a combined asset benchmark. Such capitalisation weighted benchmarks may have little relevance for many funds, however, where the general criteria for asset allocation is determined by other means. For example pension funds may determine the asset allocation guidelines from an analysis of the liabilities. In such circumstances the fund is likely to create a fund benchmark by specifying suitable proportions of the various asset classes. For example 40% Equities, 50% Bonds, 10% Real Estate may be taken as the benchmark allocation and suitable benchmark indices are selected for each asset class.

First Chicago Investment Advisors developed such a Multiple Markets Index (MMI) around 1985/6.[5] They reviewed over eighty asset classes but finally settled on nine assets which they defined as the 'investable capital market'. The proportions of each asset in the index were determined by the use of an optimisation process such that the index exhibited mean-variance characteristics similar to typical pension funds. The assets used and their proportions are shown in Table 2.9.

The main arguments for the MMI were not just to create a useful benchmark but to encourage pension funds to widen their investment horizons. The proportions incorporated in the index reflected the likely practical representation in a US pension fund and not the capitalisation of the underlying asset.

Universe benchmarks

A further development for funds is to create a universe benchmark. Such benchmarks evolved naturally during the development of the performance measurement services in the 1960s and 1970s. In providing their Funds Evaluation Service to pension fund clients, A G Becker began to publish aggregated data on the funds so measured. This aggregated data itself became a benchmark of performance for similar funds. For example the SEI Linked Median Large Plan universe became a commonly used benchmark for US Pension plans.

In the UK several of the actuaries to pension funds who had been providing valuation services to their clients pooled their resources to produce the Combined Actuarial Performance Services (CAPS). This created an aggregate of the returns provided to the individual funds. Wood Mackenzie (later to evolve as The WM Company) also provided valuation and performance measurement services and from the early 1970s produced aggregated results for their pension fund universe. That universe currently measures over 1300 funds and covers an estimated 75% of the aggregate value of UK based pension funds. The CAPS universe also measures over 1700 funds but with a lower value since the average fund size is lower.

The aggregated performance data from such universes provided a useful benchmark for pension funds so long as the fund being considered was deemed to have sufficient common characteristics with the universe. As the pension

---

[5] See 'A Composite Portfolio Benchmark for Pension Plans', *Financial Analysts Journal,* March/April 1986, Brinson, Diermeier and Schlarbaum.

fund sector developed the funds evolved more diverse characteristics and the need for more defined universes has developed.

In the USA, for example, the management structure of the funds is viewed as an important factor. Thus funds managed by the investment departments of the major banks are deemed to be different to those managed by a diverse range of specialist boutiques (perhaps under the guidance of investment consultants).

In the UK, size tended to create a different strategic asset structure so that large funds were not easily compared with smaller funds. The WM Company universe was consequently sub-divided to allow a size-related universe to be used as a benchmark if the fund so wished.

Similar considerations come into play in other universes. In the UK, again, The WM Company have produced a Charity Fund Universe but sub-divide it depending upon the constraints which might be applied to various charitable bodies.

The combinations possible when creating universes are manifold and new benchmarks are being launched on a regular basis. The important criteria are that a sufficient number and spread of funds is measured to create a good sample; that the funds have a reasonable degree of commonality; and that the users of the benchmark are satisfied to use the universe as a performance benchmark.

The issues

As the description of their evolution in this chapter illustrates, indices and benchmarks have proliferated. In some cases this is justified by the unique characteristics required of the benchmark to satisfy its purpose. In many other cases however the various benchmarks are very similar and have been developed for commercial, proprietorial reasons. Many participants argue that such proliferation serves only to confuse the end users. They would prefer a single, agreed, standard to be produced. The market needs of the participants have been and continue to be evolving rapidly, however, and it is arguable whether a monopoly supplier dependent on the formulation of an industry wide consensus would be sufficiently responsive. The competition of the commercial world may be the most effective way in which market demands can be met speedily and effectively.

For example the Capital International World Index served its purpose admirably in its early years but was considered to have several drawbacks by the time the FT/S&P–AWI series was formulated. The stimulation of that and the launch of other world indices, led to a series of major developments in the CIWI under its new guise as the Morgan Stanley Capital International index series.

Similarly the early world bond indices had restricted availability and calculation frequency but the advent of new proprietary products led to wider dissemination and more frequent calculation.

Provided the end users understand the options open to them it can be argued that the wider choice available ensures the availability of the best products. As in any other commercially competitive field, where the product is seen to be superfluous to the consumers' needs or is outshone by the competitor's products it suffers an inevitable decline and falls into disuse. Such a fate has befallen many index series over the past 100 years.

Another issue raised is that indices can be created to match the performance rather than the performance being measured against the index. This is more a matter for the various participants in the market to resolve. In some circumstances, refinements to a benchmark index may be justified by the circumstances of the portfolio or fund. Specific constraints, for example, would render comparison of a portfolio against an unrestrained benchmark to be of limited value. In other situations the manager may be seeking to amend the benchmark only to accommodate his own investment style or philosophy. Without an objective benchmark the client would be unable to evaluate the impact of that style or philosophy.

Ultimately these questions can only be resolved by the participants having a thorough understanding of the benchmarks being selected and the ultimate objective of any performance measurement process.

CHAPTER

Performance analysis

Introduction

If proper management control is to be exercised the simple measurement of performance is unlikely to be adequate. A deviation of performance from the chosen benchmark may be worthy of attention but without suitable tools for analysis to pinpoint the cause, sensible management response would be difficult.

One of the keys to effective analysis is the availability of accurate data and the facility to manipulate it effectively. Consequently the early development of performance analysis was inhibited by lack of data or the costs of collecting and processing such data.

Nevertheless the early reports by the BAI in 1968 and the SIA in 1972 recommended that the measurement of a fund's performance should also include the measurement of the performance of the separate asset classes (or sections) within the fund and their contribution to the overall fund performance. The BAI report (items 1 & 5 as detailed in Chapter 1) highlighted not only the need to measure overall rate of return and risk but also to measure performance of the separate asset classes.

The IIMR report also dealt with the components of performance but from a slightly different angle:

The Components – the performance of a fund's investments over a period of time depends upon two factors – the selection of stocks and the selection of sectors. The contribution of each of these components to the overall performance can be found by breaking down the transition from the Actual Fund (with the actual stocks chosen and the actual amounts invested in the sectors) to the Fully Restrained Fund (with the investment in the index and the Trustees' proportions) as shown below:

Source of profit/loss

Test	
Selection of stocks	Actual fund (actual investments, actual proportions minus partly restrained fund (index investment, actual proportions)
Selection of sectors	Partly restrained fund (index investment, actual proportions) minus fully restrained fund (index investment, Trustees' proportions)
Total	Actual fund (actual investments, actual proportions) minus fully restrained fund (index investment, Trustees' proportions)

In this chapter we trace the development of performance analysis and give some examples of portfolio and fund analysis in practice.

The approach to rate of return and risk

On both sides of the Atlantic general agreement on the appropriate way of measuring rate of return for comparative analysis and attribution purposes was reached. The time weighted return (TWR) was to be the effective measure of return. Despite general agreement on this issue there were still differences on the actual algorithm to be used in the calculation of the TWR. (See Chapter 5.)

On the subject of risk, however, the Atlantic proved to be a significant divide. In the USA the considerable body of academic research, particularly on equity portfolios, had evolved from the Capital Asset Pricing Model (CAPM) postulated by Sharpe.[1] In his 1965 paper Treynor had suggested the use of the 'Market Line' to evaluate mutual funds and subsequently developed this to a wider application as a means of measuring risk.

Eugene Fama authored a special supplement on risk for the BAI report of 1968, drawing on his own earlier work as well as that of Sharpe, Treynor & Jensen.[2]

All of this led to the development of specific risk adjustment factors known by their author thus:

---

[1] Capital Asset Prices: 'A Theory of Market Equilibrium Under Condition of Risk', William F Sharpe, *Journal of Finance*, September 1964.
[2] 'The Performance of Mutual Funds in the Period 1945–64', Michael C Jensen, *Journal of Finance*, May 1968.

$$\text{Treynor measure} = \frac{\text{Excess return on portfolio}}{\text{Beta on portfolio}}$$

$$\text{Sharpe measure} = \frac{\text{Excess return on portfolio}}{\text{Standard deviation of portfolio}}$$

The Jensen measure was a further development in that it did not produce a simple adjustment factor. He recognised that, despite assuming well diversified portfolios in common with Treynor and Sharpe, some portfolios might produce a regression intercept different from the origin. In terms of the regression equation therefore he had:

Excess return = Unique return + beta (Excess return+ random error
on portfolio   (alpha)   on market index)

Although applicable to equity portfolios these adjustment factors were less easy to create for other asset classes and for the total fund. Consequently in the UK they gained little currency and the IIMR simply recommended the use of total volatility in the form of the mean standard deviation of returns as a useful statistic, in line with the basic BAI recommendation.

The UK attitude to risk was reviewed and summarised in an article in *The Investment Analyst* in December 1972 by Graham Cocks.[3] To quote from that article:

The second most important element of a fund's performance is probably the level of 'risk' associated with the portfolio. However, 'risk' has been defined and measured in so many ways in the past that it may be preferable to avoid the use of the term altogether. Instead we may consider any or all of a number of factors which seem to be associated with the level of risk of a portfolio. A list of such factors would include:

1. The variability of the rate of return on the portfolio.

2. The volatility of the rate of return on the portfolio, which is its sensitivity to the rate of return on the market and is usually measured by a regression coefficient or β coefficient.

3. The relative strength of the portfolio.

4. The diversification of the portfolio.

5. The vulnerability of the portfolio, which is the probability that a minimum specified rate of return may not be achieved.

---

[3] 'An Objective Approach to the Analysis of Portfolio Performance', Graham Cocks, *The Investment Analyst*, December 1972.

Many fund managers and trustees are not interested in these secondary elements of performance, but those who are require a system of analysing portfolio performance which is flexible in that it may take these factors into account, as well as the all important rate of return.

The problem of arriving at a single measure which can reconcile the two dimensions of return and risk still remains in the UK and the major developments in performance measurement over the past 25 years have been concentrated on the return dimension and a proper analysis of achieved returns.

To quote from an article in *The Investment Analyst* by Dugald Eadie in December 1973:[4]

Without any other information about the funds concerned, if one was informed that Fund E had an average return of 10 per cent with mean deviation of 8 per cent, and Fund F had an average return of 10 per cent with mean deviation of 4 per cent, then one might be more optimistic about the chances of Fund F maintaining the return in the future.

There is an academic school of thought which goes further than this, and, using the capital asset pricing model, adjusts historical performance for risk. This adjustment then leads to the statement that Fund F is better, or more 'efficient' than Fund E because it has achieved the same return for less risk.

There is a danger in carrying this approach too far. The variability of past performance may be an indication of past riskiness, but in practical terms risk is a more direct concept. The fund manager 'takes risks' by taking certain actions (and also by not taking action). For example, he may take the risk of investing the entire fund in UK equities, or he may take the risk of holding 20 per cent of the fund in cash. The first risk will pay off if the UK equity market rises soon, while the latter risk requires the opposite. Over a period of years, the return achieved by the fund reflects the success or otherwise of these risky decisions which are continuously taken by the fund manager.

In reviewing the future expectations of Fund E and Fund F, the most important questions are:

(a) How are the funds currently structured?

(b) What is the mechanism which leads to future investment decisions?

---

[4] 'A Practical Approach to the Measurement and Analysis of Investment Performance', Dugald Eadie, *The Investment Analyst*, December 1973.

The investment manager and his Board of Trustees or Directors must be concerned with risk, and may use the variability of past performance as one indicator of past riskiness. However, their main concern is to the future, and they must continuously examine the current portfolio to gauge its exposure to risk, and should review the decision-making process to ensure that management recognise situations where risks are being taken. It is for this latter purpose that the performance analysis is a powerful tool, as it specifies the outcome of past decisions, and may perhaps indicate areas of risk-taking that are not covered explicitly by the management system.

In the UK then risk was perceived in a broader context at the fund level and a qualitative dimension was preferred to a straight quantitative approach.

Attribution analysis at asset class level

The purpose of performance analysis was to attribute the performance to the various management decisions. Ideally it should seek to establish the contribution from all levels of decision making from the basic strategic decision to allocate funds to defined asset categories down to the detailed decision to invest in specific stocks or shares. By using suitable benchmarks the relative performance attribution can also be calculated to explain the sources of any variance from benchmark performance.

At the highest level the decision by trustees to allocate funds according to a long term liability/asset model could be measured. This depends upon the establishment of some ultimate benchmark. Very often the ultimate benchmark is taken as the aggregate asset structure of a peer group universe but it could be limited to the result of the asset/liability modelling exercise itself or some other standard. Whatever the chosen benchmark the purpose is to measure the effect that any decisions attributable to the trustees might have on the performance of the fund and its variance from the benchmark.

At the next level the contribution of individual fund managers to performance is analysed. Each manager will have a benchmark specified depending upon his role within the overall fund. This can range from a very wide role (for example a single manager of a multi-asset fund with responsibility for all the investment decisions within the guidelines laid down by the trustees), to a narrowly defined role (for example a manager of a specialist equity portfolio consisting of small companies). The manager with the wider role is likely to sub-divide responsibilities down to portfolio levels and the contribution of these different elements can be measured against appropriate benchmarks.

At whatever level the principle of calculating the contribution remains the same:

Proportion of asset within total × Return on asset = Contribution of asset

	POSITIVE PERFORMANCE DIFFERENCE	NEGATIVE PERFORMANCE DIFFERENCE
OVERWEIGHT	POSITIVE CONTRIBUTION	NEGATIVE CONTRIBUTION
UNDERWEIGHT	NEGATIVE CONTRIBUTION	POSITIVE CONTRIBUTION

3.1 Contribution from asset allocation decisions.

To calculate the relative contribution, the benchmark must be incorporated into the equation.

A relative contribution can come from two possible sources:-

1. A proportion of the asset in the actual fund different from the proportion of that asset in the benchmark. This is often referred to as a policy contribution.

2. A return on the asset in the actual fund different from the return on that asset in the benchmark. This is referred to as a selection contribution.

Whether or not these deviations from the benchmark add or subtract from performance depends on the differences in weight and the differences in performance of the asset in question as illustrated in Fig. 3.1. An overweight exposure to an asset with a positive performance difference produces a positive contribution (upper left box). Thus the formula for policy contribution or the contribution from asset category allocation decisions is:

$$\begin{bmatrix} \text{Proportion of} & \text{Proportion of asset} \\ \text{asset within fund} & - & \text{within benchmark} \\ \text{at start period} & \text{at start period} \end{bmatrix} \times \begin{bmatrix} \text{Return on asset} & \text{Return on} \\ \text{within benchmark} & - & \text{benchmark} \\ \text{for period} & \text{for period} \end{bmatrix} = \begin{array}{l} \text{Policy} \\ \text{contribution} \end{array}$$

Similarly the overall selection contribution can be derived simply by:

$$\begin{bmatrix} \text{Return on asset} & \text{Return on asset} \\ \text{within fund} & - & \text{within benchmark} \\ \text{for period} & \text{for period} \end{bmatrix} \times \begin{array}{l} \text{Proportion of} \\ \text{asset within fund} = \\ \text{at start period} \end{array} \begin{array}{l} \text{Total} \\ \text{selection} \\ \text{contribution} \end{array}$$

Over most measurement periods changes will occur within the portfolio. In the absence of valuations and attribution analysis being carried out each time such a change occurs the sum of the policy contribution and the stock contribution will not equal the actual difference in performance. This is because the changes are effectively altering either the asset allocation or the stock selection. This residual number will be positive or negative depending upon how effective such changes were. They are effectively market timing decisions being taken by the manager and as such this residual number is often referred to as a TIMING or CHANGE/TIMING contribution.

Table 3.1 shows a summary attribution analysis produced by The WM Company for a demonstration fund with various international assets. The performance benchmark for the fund is the WM Universe of UK pension funds. The top half of the table shows the asset allocation of the fund compared with the benchmark at the start of the period and at the end. Changes implemented during the period are shown in the middle columns and broadly indicate the extent to which net new investment into the category has been more or less than proportionate to that category's position at the start of the period. The bottom half of the table attributes the relative performance of the fund, shown in the middle of the three boxes at the bottom, to its component parts.

The two columns to the left of the table show the contribution from policy, i.e. the asset distribution of the fund relative to the benchmark. The first of the columns shows the contribution from the initial asset mix and the second from changes undertaken through the period relative to the universe.

The total initial policy contribution is 1.7% with two important contributions (0.6%) coming from the relative exposure to Total Pacific (ex Japan) and UK Property. The top half of the table shows that the fund had a high relative exposure in Total Pacific (ex Japan) and a low relative exposure to UK Property. The extreme right hand column in the bottom half of the table shows the universe returns from these areas, +37.5% and –1.3% respectively. The total universe return was 18.6% (bottom left hand box).

The fund therefore gained performance from being overweight in a relatively strong performing asset (37.5% vs 18.6%) and underweight in a relatively weak performing asset (–1.3% vs 18.6%). The same applied, to a lesser degree, to the fund's relative holdings in Overseas Bonds and Cash.

The policy contribution from CHANGE/TIMING was close to neutral overall with small positives arising from the relative shifts in exposure in North America and Continental Europe offset by small negatives from the move into UK Equities, Cash and Overseas Bonds relative to the universe. (Note:- although UK Equities and Overseas Bonds showed relative strength over the whole period the negative change/timing contributions indicate that these assets showed relative weakness over the period following the extra investment.)

The right hand columns in the bottom half of the table show the contribution from selection within the asset classes (where the asset class is restricted to a single market this would be the stock selection effect, where the asset class includes several markets, e.g. Continental Europe, this would combine both market and stock selection).

Table 3.1 Summary attribution analysis

Year to Dec 1992

UK PENSIONS - WM ALL FUNDS

ASSET MIX

INVESTMENT CATEGORY	% INITIAL MARKET VALUE		% POLICY CHANGE		% FINAL MARKET VALUE	
	FUND	WM UNIVERSE	FUND	WM UNIVERSE	FUND	WM UNIVERSE
UK Equities	62	56	2	0	64	58
Overseas Equities	27	21	-5	-0	24	22
North America	6	6	0	-1	7	6
Continental Europe	11	8	-4	0	8	8
Japan	4	5	-1	-0	2	4
Total Pacific (Ex Japan)	6	2	0	0	7	3
Other Intl Equities		1		-0		0
UK Bonds	0	5	0	-0	0	4
Overseas Bonds	6	4	2	0	8	4
UK Index-Linked		2		0		3
Cash/Other Investments	0	4	1	0	1	4
UK Property	4	7	0	-0	3	6
Overseas Property	0	1	0	0		1
TOTAL ASSETS INC PROPERTY	FUND INITIAL VALUE (£'m) 178		FUND NET INVESTMENT (£'M) -1		FUND FINAL VALUE (£'M) 216	

ATTRIBUTION

POLICY			SELECTION			
INITIAL	CHANGE TIMING	INVESTMENT CATEGORY	WEIGHTED CONTRIBUTION	% RETURN		
					FUND	WM UNIVERSE
0.1	-0.1	UK Equities	3.2		26.9	20.8
0.6	0.2	Overseas Equities	1.6		30.5	19.7
-0.0	0.1	North America		0.5	42.5	32.4
0.0	0.1	Continental Europe		0.4	21.8	18.3
0.0	0.0	Japan		0.0	-0.9	-0.9
0.6	-0.0	Total Pacific (Ex Japan)		0.6	51.7	37.5
-0.0	0.0	Other Intl Equities				21.0
-0.0	0.0	UK Bonds	0.0		31.4	19.1
0.2	-0.1	Overseas Bonds	-0.0		27.9	29.1
0.0	0.0	UK Index-Linked				17.8
0.1	-0.1	Cash/Other Investments	-0.0		9.2	13.2
0.6	-0.0	UK Property	0.3		7.4	-1.3
0.1	0.0	Overseas Property	-0.1		n/a	0.8
1.7	-0.0		4.9			

18.6	6.7	26.5

The relative performance within the asset class is weighted by the average exposure of the asset during the period to produce the weighted contribution from SELECTION.

The total selection contribution for the fund was 4.9% coming mainly from the relative performance in the two main equity categories. The fund produced a relative return in UK equities of 5.0% $\left[\left(\dfrac{126.9}{120.8} - 1\right) \times 100 = 5.05\%\right]$ which weighted by an average asset exposure of 63% produced a weighted contribution of 3.2%. In Overseas Equities the contribution of 1.6% must be derived by multiplying the individual asset class contributions and not from the overall relative return on Overseas Equities. The main contributions came from strong relative returns in North America, Continental Europe and Total Pacific (ex Japan).

The other notable contribution came from UK Property where the relative return of 8.8% added a further 0.3% to the selection total.

Multiplying the contribution totals $\left(\dfrac{101.7 \times 104.9}{100} = 106.7\right)$ produces the overall relative performance of the fund of 6.7% $\left[\left(\dfrac{126.5}{118.6} - 1\right) \times 100 = 6.66\%\right]$

For the period in question the fund trustees or plan sponsor now has an analysis of the relative return of the fund with considerable extra information as to the sources of that performance. It may be that the trustees are themselves responsible for the basic asset allocation decisions in which case they can be credited with a positive contribution. The fund may be split between several specialists, managing the UK equities, Pacific Basin, fixed interest, etc, in which case each can be seen to make their own contribution.

More detailed analysis can be carried out on the specialist portfolios against their own specified benchmarks.

The added benefit of the multiplicative attribution analysis is that all the contributions can be compounded across investment areas and time frames. Thus longer term analysis can be carried out along the lines shown in Table 3.2.

Attribution within asset class – Equities

This type of attribution analysis can be carried down to whatever level of detail is required, dependent only on the availability of data. Thus the attribution of selection can be broken down to individual stocks within an equity portfolio, or industry sector. In his article in *The Investment Analyst* of December 1973 Dugald Eadie provided a worked example of this type of tiered attribution analysis as applied to an equity portfolio. It is reproduced in full as Appendix 2.

Table 3.2 Long term attribution analysis

Long Term Attribution

YEAR	1983	1984	1985	1986	1987	1988	1989	1990	1991	1992	5 YRS	3 YRS
WM UNIVERSE RETURN				22.5	3.4	13.8	30.3	-10.6	16.9	18.6	13.0	7.4
YOUR FUND'S RETURN				25.0	1.7	13.6	36.8	-9.5	20.3	26.5	16.4	11.3
RELATIVE RETURN				2.0	-1.7	-0.2	5.0	1.2	2.9	6.7	3.0	3.6
Attributed to:												
POLICY				1.8	0.4	-0.2	1.8	-1.2	1.5	1.7	0.7	0.7
Change/Timing				-0.0	1.6	-0.3	-0.6	-1.3	-0.4	-0.0	-0.6	-0.6
UK Equities				0.2	0.2	-0.3	0.4	-		0.1	0.1	0.1
Overseas Equities				0.5	-0.7	-0.2	0.2	0.6	0.5	0.6	0.4	0.5
North America								-0.4	0.2	-		-0.1
Continental Europe								-1.0	-0.1	-		0.3
Japan								1.8	0.1	-		0.5
Total Pacific (Ex Japan)									0.3	0.6	-	0.3
Other Intl Equities								0.2	-	-		0.0
UK Bonds				0.3	-0.4	0.3	1.7	-1.2	-0.1	-	0.2	-0.4
Overseas Bonds				-	-	0.1	0.1	-0.2	0.3	0.2	0.1	0.1
UK Index-Linked				0.5	-0.1	-	0.9	1.5	0.2	-	0.1	0.5
Cash/Other Investments				-	-	0.2	0.4	-0.5	0.2	0.1	0.1	-0.0
UK Property				0.2	-0.3	-0.3	0.5	-0.2	0.7	0.6	0.2	0.4
Overseas Property				0.2	-	-	0.5	-	0.1	0.1	0.0	0.1

'-' represents a figure of less than 0.05 and greater than -0.5

SELECTION	0.2	-2.0	-0.1	3.1	2.5	1.4	4.9	2.4	2.9
UK Equities	-0.4	1.6	0.6	2.0	1.7	1.8	3.2	1.9	2.2
Overseas Equities	0.5	-2.4	-0.5	1.1	0.6	-0.7	1.6	0.4	0.5
North America					-0.2	-0.1	0.5		0.1
Continental Europe					0.6	-0.1	0.4		0.3
Japan					0.1	-0.1	-		-0.0
Total Pacific (Ex Japan)						-0.5	0.6		0.1
Other Intl Equities						-	-		
UK Bonds	-	0.1	0.1	-	-	-	-	0.0	0.0
Overseas Bonds		-	-		-0.5	0.2	-	-0.0	-0.1
UK Index-Linked		-0.1	-	0.1	-0.1	-	-	-0.0	-0.0
Cash/Other Investments	-	-	-0.1	-	-	0.1	-	-0.0	0.0
UK Property	0.3	-0.8	0.3	-	0.7	-0.1	0.3	0.2	0.3
Overseas Property	-	-0.3	-0.4	-	-	-	-0.1	-0.1	-0.0

'-' represents a figure of less than 0.05 and greater than -0.05

Source : The WM Company

Within equities the attribution analysis aims to identify the contribution to performance from sector selection and, within sectors, from stock selection. The impact of the timing of any actions can also be quantified.

In the example shown in Appendix 2 the equity sectors are classified along the lines of the FT–SE–A All Share Index industrial classification. The sector classification might equally be made along the lines of size (e.g. FT–SE 100, FT–SE 250, Smaller Companies). Alternatively the market might be classified by other 'style' characteristics which has become popular in the USA (e.g. growth, income, cyclical).

Barra International developed a form of factor analysis based on a multiple regression of the equities within a market. This identifies certain economic and market variables which have determined the price response of shares. Portfolio analysis can then be carried out to attribute portfolio performance to the relative exposure of the portfolio to these variables or factors. Unlike the analysis by industrial sector or style, factor analysis does not allow the impact of stock selection within the factor to be calculated since stocks are not exclusive to a factor in the way that they are exclusive to an individual sector or style. Current developments in this area are examined in Section Four.

Attribution within asset class – Bonds

The same principles of attribution analysis can be used for any asset category provided the data is suitably presented. In the USA, where bond portfolio analysis is more common due to the extensive and varied nature of the bond market, attribution analysis takes on a different aspect. This is because the division of the bond market is along very different lines to that of the equity market. A portfolio may be viewed in several different ways depending upon the approach of the manager, or plan sponsor.

The division of the portfolio can be on the basis of duration (i.e. sensitivity to interest rate changes), maturity (i.e. years to redemption), coupon/yield (i.e. high, medium or low yields) or by default risk (i.e. investment grade bonds or 'junk' bonds).

The availability of benchmark indices covering most combinations was discussed in Chapter 2 (Merrill Lynch for example) so that attribution analysis can be carried out to show the contribution from being in a particular sector of the market or a particular stock within a sector. Table 3.3 shows the style universes used in the past by Frank Russell Company and the appropriate benchmark index. Figure 3.2 shows how universe data might typically be presented.

A normal or notional fund can be created by allocating proportions to suitable benchmark indices.

Table 3.3 Example of US fixed-income style universes

Style	Comparison Indexes
Active duration accounts	Shearson Lehman Hutton (SLH) Aggregate
	SLH Government/Corporate
Active sector rotation accounts	SLH Aggregate
	SLH Government/Corporate
Intermediate bond accounts	SLH Intermediate Government/Corporate
Long-term bond accounts	SLH Long-Term Government/Corporate
Short-intermediate bond accounts	Merrill Lynch 1-2.99 Years Treasury Master
	Payden & Rygel 2-Year Treasury Notes
Short-term investment fund (STIF)	Salomon Bros. 6-Month Treasury Bills
and cash accounts	Commercial Paper
Convertible securities accounts	First Boston Convertible
	Goldman Sachs 100 Convertible
	Froley, Revy 30 Convertible
High-yield bond accounts	SLH Government/Corporate
	Salomon Bros. High-Yield Corporate
Municipal bond accounts	SLH Municipal

Source: Frank Russell Company

Attribution within asset class – Other assets

Attribution analysis is most prevalent within equity and bond portfolios but the development of comprehensive databanks on property or real estate has enabled more detailed analysis to be carried out on these portfolios. IPD, in the UK, for example identify the different returns produced by property on both a geographic basis and a functional basis (office, retail, industrial). Portfolios can thus be analysed to show the attribution to relative return from relative exposure to those classifications.

In effect the scope for performance analysis is limited only by the availability of suitable data and the acceptable classification of the asset class.

A Universe Quartile Chart showing Return Quartiles and Comparisons with relevant Bond Index returns for Active Duration Accounts for periods ending September 30th, 1988

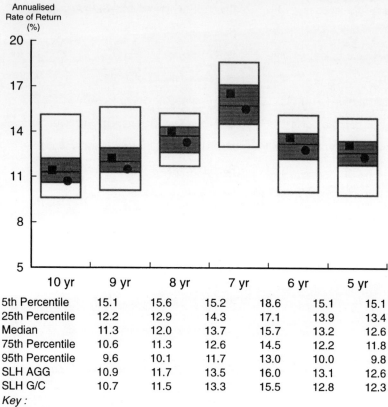

	10 yr	9 yr	8 yr	7 yr	6 yr	5 yr
5th Percentile	15.1	15.6	15.2	18.6	15.1	15.1
25th Percentile	12.2	12.9	14.3	17.1	13.9	13.4
Median	11.3	12.0	13.7	15.7	13.2	12.6
75th Percentile	10.6	11.3	12.6	14.5	12.2	11.8
95th Percentile	9.6	10.1	11.7	13.0	10.0	9.8
SLH AGG	10.9	11.7	13.5	16.0	13.1	12.6
SLH G/C	10.7	11.5	13.3	15.5	12.8	12.3

Key :

■ SLH AGG = Shearson Lehman Hutton Aggregate Bond Index

● SLH G/C = Shearson Lehman Hutton Government/Corporate Index

Source : Frank Russell Company

3.2 Sample quartile chart.

The issues

It can be argued that producing detailed analysis of the type described in this chapter and appendices serves to confuse the trustees and can do little to influence future performance. Poring over past figures of returns which are, by definition, historic is just a form of 'data mining' and the outcome just statistical mumbo-jumbo.

Whilst it is true that the experience of the past is unlikely to be exactly repeated in the future it remains important to analyse the source of past performance and to build up a history so that characteristics can be identified. Given so much data there is a temptation to 'data mine' but this does not apply where specific management information with a specific end purpose is being sought.

In order to build up the sort of history which may be valuable, however, frequent observations must be made which implies short time periods. Does this lead to 'short-termism' in the management of the funds? The answer has to be that it can, if there is not a clear understanding of the purpose of the data by both manager and trustee. Monthly or quarterly data may be necessary to build a statistically significant data series but it should not be used to make judgements on performance over those same time periods. Indeed the purpose of building the database is to enable analysis and subsequent judgements to be carried out on longer term results.

Three years of results, with at least quarterly data, can be regarded as a minimum time frame. Even so critics may argue that it is impossible to distinguish skill from luck. Statistically that may be a valid judgement but it is likely to need a lifetime of observations before statistically significant results might be produced.

The interpretation of performance analysis data has to come with suitable warnings, therefore, and qualitative judgements might be as important as quantitative ones. It is also vital that the type and detail of the analysis has some relevance to the management process and the terms of reference of the portfolio manager.

Management control

Introduction

In the previous chapter the issue was raised of whether or not hindsight data has any use in the exercise of management control. Although past events will not necessarily repeat themselves the answer must be that some knowledge, albeit of historic events, is better than no knowledge.

Information on past performance can be used pro-actively and re-actively depending upon the user and the purpose to which the information is put. In this chapter we look at the ways in which performance data is used.

Fund management promotion

For many years the past performance of a fund has been used by fund managers to promote their business. From the early launch of open-ended mutual funds or unit trusts the record of the fund has been presented in promotional literature.

Very often such promotion was presented in a form designed to flatter past performance. For example the growth of the fund might be compared with the FT Industrial Ordinary Index. As described in Chapter 2, over time such an index would inevitably underperform a capitalisation weighted arithmetic index. Such practices were not necessarily used to deceive deliberately; until 1962 the FT Industrial Ordinary Index was, probably, the most widely quoted benchmark of UK market performance. Funds would also be promoted showing returns over particular time periods, usually chosen to reflect the fund performance in the most favourable light. Similarly, fund management organisations might promote their skills using selected funds which could present their results in the most favourable light. Such simplistic use of historic performance data might be regarded as misleading rather than informative.

It was for this reason that performance measurement standards were evolved. In addition the development of better techniques of performance analysis allowed a better understanding of the characteristics of the performance.

The growth of the mutual fund industry in the USA during the fifties and sixties, with its attendant competitive claims from the management companies, prompted much of the research which led to the evolution of the Capital Asset Pricing Model and other investment concepts. The work published by Jenson, Sharpe, Treynor et al in the sixties was based on mutual fund data. Treynor, for example, was concerned, in his 1965 paper 'How to Rate Management of Investment Funds' , with the fact that the apparent performance rankings might be the result of fund characteristics rather than management skill. Without such historic performance data and suitable analysis it would be impossible to make useful judgements and exercise management control.

Over the past thirty years the industry has evolved a series of standards, both formal and informal, which evolve from three basic concepts applied to assessing fund MANAGEMENT performance.

- A suitable benchmark should be established i.e. one which is a relevant reflection of the aims and objectives of the fund.

- Time weighted returns should be calculated to isolate fund MANAGEMENT skills from the impact of factors outside management control such as cash flows.

- Total returns should be used to identify the overall wealth effect.

The benchmark might be an established index, a specifically structured index or a universe or peer group of funds.

When reviewing the promotional material of fund managers these basic rules should be borne in mind. Where practicable the numbers used should be provided by, or audited by, independent measurers. (Chapter 7 looks in more detail at standards.) Given these safeguards the use of historic performance data can provide useful information to investors in the exercise of their investment choices and management control.

Managing the managers

For the investor the main purpose of gathering and analysing historic performance data is to exercise judgement on the effectiveness of the fund managers. From the initial choice of manager through the ongoing monitoring of performance to the ultimate sanction of firing the manager (or selling the fund), the investor needs the data on which to make judgements and informed decisions, and performance analysis is an important part of such data.

Selection

Although by no means the only factor in the selection process there is little doubt that past performance is a powerful one. Despite evidence that superior performance is hard to sustain and very hard to identify in advance (see Chapter 9) there are powerful pressures to choose managers with recent track records of success. One influential reason is that where the person or persons responsible for the decision is accountable to others it is easier, in the event of subsequent performance being disappointing, to justify the choice of a previously successful manager than of a previously unsuccessful one.

This is particularly relevant where outside consultants are employed to advise on manager selection. The development of 'league tables' becomes inevitable and it is important that they are not accepted at their face value.

Even if they are compiled in accordance with the three concepts listed earlier, a fuller analysis of the performance should throw valuable light on the problem of selection. How volatile has the performance been? Is it the result of one or two large but successful positions taken over a particular period? Does it reflect a disciplined and repeatable methodology? Is it the result of a particular style? Only a full analysis of the results (and the organisation) can answer these questions. But without the data on performance they could not be answered at all and valid management decisions would be impossible.

Consultants, who assist in the management selection process, now carry out comprehensive and detailed analysis of the performance of the fund managers to answer these questions. Without performance measurement and analysis the task of sensible manager selection would be impossible.

Monitoring

Having appointed a manager, or bought shares in a fund, continued monitoring of the performance is essential if responsible management decisions are to be made. At the basic level the returns achieved by the fund must be measured and compared with the objectives. Failure to meet objectives may call for some changes to be made if it can be demonstrated that they could have been met with alternative strategies. The returns from such alternative strategies therefore need to be monitored for comparative purposes. Since there may be infinite alternative strategies this is usually restricted to a limited number of specific benchmarks such as indices or universes of other funds.

The time intervals over which such monitoring is conducted depends upon the individual fund and the nature of the management control to be exercised. Even where the time interval for active management decisions is long, the performance measurement interval may need to be short in order to build up data. This is particularly relevant where the monitoring process involves elements of quantitative or statistical analysis. Such analysis requires a minimum number of observations or data values to be statistically valid and, therefore, useful. Conducting the measurement process over short time intervals does not, necessarily, imply 'short-termism' on the part of the investor. The producer of motor cars has a clear long term commitment to his investment but he will still measure output and efficiency, probably on a daily basis!

Data on performance can thus highlight deviations from the standard and can be supported by other information to enable a proper analysis of such deviations to be conducted. The ultimate purpose of such information is to allow management to function efficiently. This applies to the direct management of the assets and to the ultimate managers – the plan sponsors, trustees or individual investors.

For the direct manager the value of performance measurement and analysis is in providing information about the characteristics of the investments which may require him to modify the mix in order to meet the objectives more effectively. For example the deviation from benchmark may be due to over or under exposure to particular types of assets. Shifts in the asset mix can be made to the fund accordingly.

For the trustee or plan sponsor the information may be used to redefine the manager's brief. The performance may have been too volatile for comfort or too much of the achieved return may have come from an asset which is regarded as too risky or unacceptable on other grounds.

The analysis of performance can help in understanding the characteristics of the fund and lead to more clearly defined expectations. This itself may lead to a redefinition of targets or benchmarks. The fund might be fragmented – to diversify management risk – or consolidated.

Changing the manager

Ultimately the analysis of performance may lead to a conclusion that the management has been unsatisfactory and needs to be changed. It is important to stress the need for analysis in this respect since the actual performance might be attributable to many factors, some of which are outside management control. Failure to meet objectives may not, therefore, be attributable to the manager. Indeed the objectives themselves may be at fault and only a full and proper analysis of the fund performance and the performance of other universes or benchmarks can provide the information upon which sensible management decisions can be taken. Changing managers can be an expensive process and needs to be properly substantiated if trustees or plan sponsors are to be seen to exercise their responsibilities effectively.

The issues

The provision of so much data on performance might be thought to be a classic case of over-kill. Analysis is being carried out for its own sake with little real benefit to the practical management of the fund. Costs have also to be considered. Although data processing costs are much less than in the past, thus making information available more cost effectively, the collection of data can still be an expensive process (see Chapter 6 – Practicalities of data collection). The temptation to 'data mine' – to pore over data until it reveals some information however irrelevant to the management process it might be in practical terms – is always present.

These are potential criticisms of the practitioners rather than of the process, however. Good management will ensure that relevant information is made available on a basis which balances the cost with the benefits.

More contentious is the issue of whether or not the results from investment management are entirely random, in which case management decisions taken on the strength of past data are valueless. But only by the process of performance measurement and analysis can such a fact be established in the first instance. If, indeed, results are random that itself can provide valuable management information. Some funds are managed on just such a contention with no effort made to impose subjective management judgement on the portfolio. Even this process requires some historic performance data, however, and benchmarks need to be monitored to ensure that they reflect the universe of investment opportunity.

Few observers now seriously question the need for performance measurement and analysis. The complexity of the process has increased over the years, however, as information technology has widened the horizons. The case for why performance is measured is well established and the problems associated with how it is measured remain complex. This subject is discussed in Section Two.

How to measure performance

In this section the measurement of performance is tackled at a practical level. Having discussed what performance measurement is we address the practical problems involved in carrying out the process. The basic calculations involved in producing a rate of return for a fund are covered in Chapter 5.

Even with an agreed formula, differences in calculated results can arise because of variations in the basic data used. The problems arising from data are covered in Chapter 6 including the problems raised by non-liquid assets and new market instruments. Chapter 7 deals with the establishment of standards, the definition of terms and the uses and pitfalls of 'league tables'.

Finally in this section we examine the question of risk in more detail. What is risk and how can it be measured satisfactorily? Can it be incorporated into performance returns or should it be separately analysed and assessed?

The basic calculations

Introduction

The concept of using more than one rate of return methodology to cover different scenarios has been introduced earlier. In this chapter the measurement of performance at a practical level is discussed and the most commonly used formulae are defined.

Money weighted and time weighted returns

The two main return calculations are known as money weighted return (MWR), often referred to as 'dollar weighted', and time weighted return (TWR). The difference between these methodologies is important to understand and indeed is key to interpreting the calculated returns.

MWR

The MWR is the actual return achieved in the asset class and is calculated based on using a simplified internal rate of return formula – discarding the second order and above terms. It uses the initial valuation of the asset, the cash flows that occur during the period and the final valuation at the end of the period. It is defined as:

$$MWR = \frac{\text{Capital gain} + \text{income}}{\text{Average capital employed}} = \frac{V_n - V_o - NI + I}{V_o + \Sigma\left(NI_i\left(1-t\right)\right)}$$

where:

V_n = Market value at the end of the period

V_o = Market value at the beginning of the period

NI = Total new money received during the period

I   = Income received during the period

Ni_i = ith cash flow

t_i = proportion of the period attributable to NI_i

This method of approximating the return using day weighted cash flows was introduced by Dietz (1966) and is known as the modified Dietz method. The formula is often simplified by estimating the average capital employed and making the assumption that 'on average' the net investment is received half way through the period. The adjusted formula is then:

$$MWR = \frac{V_n - V_o - NI + I}{V_o + 1/2(NI)}$$

This version of the formula was used historically when the input data was manually prepared and therefore involved the supply of only four items of data. However, this method is prone to statistically significant errors when the cash flows relative to the assets held are large and occur unevenly over the period.

A simple example demonstrates. Let us assume that an asset is valued on day 1 at $1000 and on day 31 at $1550. There is a cash flow in the asset on day 6 of $400. Using the simplified version of the formula the return would be calculated as:

$$MWR = \frac{1550 - 1000 - 400}{1000 + 1/2(400)} = \frac{150}{1200} = 12.5\%$$

Using the accurate dating of the cash flow would give:

$$MWR = \frac{1550 - 1000 - 400}{1000 + 25/31(400)} = \frac{150}{1323} = 11.3\%$$

A number of variations of the MWR calculation are often used. One is to use a combination of the above when calculating the average capital employed, where the significant cash flows are specifically dated (e.g. those greater than 5% of the initial valuation of the asset) and the remainder are aggregated and assumed to have occurred at the midway point of the period. Another method is to aggregate all the cash flows for the period and apply them to the most appropriate date i.e. a day weighted average. If we had a cash flow of $100 on day 6 and $1000 on day 25 in a 31 day period then this could be interpreted as $1100 being added to day 23.27.

Whilst the MWR is the true return of the asset, it includes the impact of the timing of the cash flows and therefore cannot be used to compare the relative performance of two managers. As the cash flows at the total fund level are normally outside the control of the manager of the assets, and will vary from one fund to another, it is important to have a more consistent measure when trying to compare the performance across funds. It is in these cases that the time weighted return is considered.

TWR

The true TWR of an asset requires the asset to be revalued at the point of each cash flow. These returns are then compounded together to form the TWR for the whole period. In effect a weighted average of sub period internal rates of return between cash flows is generated. However, this method has the drawback of having to capture all the data at the point of each cash flow, in particular the need for the asset revaluation causes significant problems. It is this method that is used for mutual fund performance – the need to calculate daily unit prices means that the required data is available. However, for most performance measurement systems the asset revaluation was not easily available. Therefore it has long been accepted to calculate an estimated TWR by combining sub period MWRs. The basic minimum period is one month i.e. a one month TWR equates to the one month MWR, and the quarterly TWR is the combination of the three monthly MWRs. This has more recently been refined through the AIMR (The Association for Investment Management and Research) standards, in the United States, to recommend that intra month valuations are supplied where 'significant' cash flows have occurred and these intra months are then compounded to create a more accurate estimate of the TWR.

The method of compounding sub-period returns to create longer period returns is often referred to as 'chainlinking'. The formula is defined as:

$$\text{TWR} = [\Pi(1 + R_i/100) - 1] \times 100$$

The $(1 + R_i/100)$ form of the return is known as its multiplicative form.

Assuming returns of 10%, 5% and 15% have been calculated over three consecutive months, then the quarterly return would be calculated as follows:

$$\text{Quarterly TWR} = ((1 + 10/100) \times (1 + 5/100) \times (1 + 15/100) - 1)) \times 100$$
$$= 32.8\%$$

This method is used to combine any number of returns over any time period. However, it is normal to make one further adjustment when the time period extends over one year – that of annualising the return. This is done by applying the following formula:

Annualised return = nth root (multiplicative compounded return)

where n is defined as = $\dfrac{\text{number of time periods}}{\text{frequency of returns}}$

For example if a fund has achieved three annual returns of 10%, 5% and 15%, then the three year annualised return is:

$$\text{nth root} = \frac{\text{number of time periods}}{\text{frequency of returns}} = \frac{3}{1}$$

$$\text{3 year annualised} = [3\sqrt{(1.328\%)} - 1] \times 100$$

$$= 9.92\%$$

For a fund with quarterly returns, the frequency of returns would be equal to 4, and for a series of monthly returns, the frequency would equal 12.

Comparison of MWR and TWR

An example of two funds with differing cash flows fully demonstrates the differences between the MWR and the TWR, and why TWRs are used to compare performance across funds.

Consider two portfolios, A and B, which move in line with an index. The index starts at 100, moves to 108 one-third of the way through the period, to 120 two-thirds of the way through, and finishes at 115 at the end of the period. To simplify the example there is no income. The rate of return of the index is therefore 15%. What are the returns of the portfolios?

Portfolios A and B are assumed to start the period at a value of 1000. Portfolio A receives 240 of new money to invest and Portfolio B receives 960 of new money, both at the top of the market i.e. two-thirds of the way through the period.

Using the formula previously defined the MWR can be calculated:

Portfolio A:

Initial market value $= I_0 \quad = 1000$

Final market value $= I_3 \quad = 1380$

New money $\quad = NI \quad = 240$

Income $\quad = I \quad = 0$

$$MWR = \frac{I_3 - I_0 - NI + I}{I_0 + \Sigma(NI_i(1 - t_i))}$$

$$= \frac{1380 - 1000 - 240 + 0}{1000 + 240 \times 1/3}$$

$$= 13.0\%$$

Portfolio B:

Initial market value $= I_0 \quad = 1000$

Final market value $= I_3 \quad = 2070$

60

New money $\qquad = NI \quad = 960$

Income $\qquad\qquad = I \quad\ = 0$

$$MWR = \frac{I_3 - I_0 - NI + I}{I_0 + \Sigma\left(NI_i\left(1 - t_i\right)\right)}$$

$$= \frac{2070 - 1000 - 960 + 0}{1000 + \left(960 \times 1/3\right)}$$

$$= 8.3\%$$

The TWR is calculated by splitting the period into two parts – the period before the cash flow and that after, calculating the MWR for each sub-period, and then chainlinking to give the full period TWR. The returns for the first period up to the cash flow are the same for both Portfolio A and B.

Portfolios A and B:

Initial market value $= I_0 \quad = 1000$

Final market value $\ = I_2 \quad = 1200$

New money $\qquad = NI \ = 0$

Income $\qquad\qquad = I \quad = 0$

$$MWR_1 = \frac{I_2 - I_0 - NI + I}{I_0 + \Sigma\left(NI_i\left(1 - t_i\right)\right)}$$

$$= \frac{1200 - 1000 - 0 + 0}{1000 + 0}$$

$$= 20.0\%$$

Looking at the second period after the cash flow:

Portfolio A:

Initial market value $= I_2 \quad = 1200$

Final market value $\ = I_3 \quad = 1380$

New money $\qquad = NI \ = 240$

Income $\qquad\qquad = I \quad = 0$

$$MWR_2 = \frac{I_3 - I_2 - NI + I}{I_2 + \Sigma\left(NI_i\left(1 - t_i\right)\right)}$$

$$= \frac{1380 - 1200 - 240 + 0}{1200 + (240 \times 1)}$$

$$= -4.2\%$$

Portfolio B:

Initial market value $= I_2 \quad = 1200$

Final market value $= I_3 \quad = 2070$

New money $\quad = NI \quad = 960$

Income $\quad\quad = I \quad = 0$

$$MWR_2 = \frac{I_3 - I_2 - NI + I}{I_2 + \Sigma(NI_i(1 - t_i))}$$

$$= \frac{2070 - 1200 - 960 + 0}{1200 + (960 \times 1)}$$

$$= -4.2\%$$

The TWR for Portfolio A and B is then:

TWR $= [(1 + 0.2) \times (1 - 0.042) - 1] \times 100 = 15.0\%$

This proves that on a time weighted basis each portfolio is performing in line with the index (15%) whereas the actual money weighted returns are quite different (13% and 8.3%).

The 'Analysts Test'

The above analysis assumed that compounding MWRs was a good approximation to the TWR, however as mentioned earlier, distortions can occur even with the day dating of cash flows. One method favoured to provide a better estimate to the TWR is that of the 'Analysts Test', defined in the IIMR report of 1972. It uses an adjustment to the MWR by defining a comparable index or benchmark for the asset, calculating a MWR of the index by applying the portfolio's cash flows to that index and assuming the relationship of the index MWR to the (known) index TWR is approximately the same as that of the portfolio's MWR to its 'true' TWR. This is defined as:

$$\frac{1 + TWR_{portfolio}}{1 + MWR_{portfolio}} = \frac{1 + TWR_{index}}{1 + MWR_{index}}$$

or equivalently

$$1 + TWR_{portfolio} = (1 + MWR_{portfolio}) \times \left(\frac{1 + TWR_{index}}{1 + MWR_{index}} \right)$$

Assume an index and portfolio move in line:

	1 June	6 June	30 June
Index	100	130	120
Portfolio	£1000	£400	£1550

The TWR for the index is straightforward.

$$TWR_I = 20\%$$

The MWR for the portfolio is:

$$MWR_p = \frac{1550 - 1400}{1000 + (25/30 \times 400)} = \frac{150}{1333} = 11.3\%$$

The MWR for the index can now be calculated using the portfolio's cash flow:

$$MWR_I = \frac{1569^* - 1400}{1333} = \frac{169}{1333} = 12.7\%$$

* this is final market value of the index fund and is calculated from:

$$£1000 \times \frac{120}{100} + £400 \times \frac{120}{130} = 1200 + 369 = 1569$$

Applying the 'Analysts Test' gives :

$$\frac{1 + TWR_p}{1 + MWR_p} = \frac{1 + TWR_I}{1 + MWR_I}$$

$$1 + TWR_p = 1.113 \times \frac{1.2}{1.127}$$

$$TWR_p = 18.5\%$$

As the table below shows the 'Analysts Test' produces a more accurate return for the portfolio than if the MWR estimate was used.

	TWR	MWR
Index	20%	12.7%
Portfolio	18.5%	11.3%

This formula should only be used when a comparable index is available for a given asset and is particularly useful when looking at index funds.

All the formulae so far have assumed a single asset class. When calculating the total portfolio or fund return, or sub-totals, the most common technique used is to combine all the raw data and apply the same formula as if it was just another asset class. Another method is to use a weighted average approach, where the per cent weights in each asset class are applied to the asset class return and added together. This, however, is very dependent on what is used as the per cent weight, e.g. the average capital employed or the opening capital employed.

Over the years access to more accurate data has become available because of the advances in computer technology and the accounting systems supplying the data. The introduction of dated cash flows into the above formulae is evidence of this. Calculating a true TWR by revaluing the portfolio after each cash flow and compounding the resulting returns is already done for mutual funds and is increasingly becoming commonplace as systems are replaced and enhanced. However, no matter how 'theoretically correct' systems become there will always be the need for judgement and interpretation of the results.

Practical issues relating to calculation of returns

The above formulae appear simple when calculating a single asset which has a beginning and ending value together with some investment. However, this is not always the case. Some typical scenarios are:

- *where the net investment into/out of the asset is large compared with the value of the asset.* It is crucial that the net investment is day dated to reduce the distortion.

- *buying into or selling from an asset class.* This in effect is a part period return. Care must be taken when looking at this return with other asset classes within the portfolio.

- *the return formulae are very sensitive to the amount of average capital employed used in the denominator. Obviously as this becomes close to zero the return can be distorted.* An example of this would be in an 'almost sell-out' situation, e.g. asset valued at 1000, sell 999 on day 1 of the period, asset valued at 2 at end of period – what is the return for the period? The formula would calculate it as 100%!

- *total portfolio returns can appear inconsistent with individual segment returns.* This often happens when there are major shifts between asset classes.

Taking the example:

	Equities		Bonds		Total portfolio
	wt	return, %	wt	return, %	return, %
January	75	4	25	−5	1.75
February	60	−3.5	40	3	−0.9
March	35	4	65	4	4

The quarterly returns would be :

Total portfolio   4.6%
Equities   4.3%
Bonds   1.3%

That is the total portfolio return is outside the asset class returns.

– *the classification of stocks into asset classes in global portfolios is not always standard.* The various index suppliers often classify stocks differently. Care must taken therefore when comparing returns.

Attribution analysis

The calculation of the return is in some ways only the beginning in the analysis of the performance of portfolios. Once the return is known the obvious question asked is:

'How does this return compare against the benchmark?'

This is known as the portfolio's relative return and is defined as:

$$Re\,lative\ return = \left[\frac{(1 + \text{Portfolio return} / 100)}{(1 + \text{Benchmark return} / 100)} - 1\right] \times 100$$

Following on from this is the question:

'How was the relative performance achieved?' This is known as performance attribution.

Performance attribution attempts to identify and quantify the effects of the managers' investment decisions. Following on from the evolving sophistication of return calculations, recent interest has moved to attribution, where a host of articles have put forward proposals for the analysis of returns to cope with the ever increasing complexities of investment instruments and the variety of different ways portfolios are being managed. There is no such thing as the definitive attribution method to cover all eventualities. In this chapter the basic approaches will be covered, indicating any limitations in the approach and briefly looking forward to where the analysis of attribution is going in the future.

As defined earlier in Chapter 4 a simple terms attribution analysis breaks down the relative return into two components:

Policy – the effect of being over- or under-weight in an investment market compared to the benchmark.

Selection – the effect of over- or under-performing the benchmark in a given market.

These can be defined as:

$$\text{Policy} = [(W^P - W^B) \times (1 + R^B /100)/(1 + R^{BT}/100) - 1] \times 100$$

$$\text{Selection} = [(W^P/PMC) \times (1 + R^P /100) - (1 + R^B/100)] \times 100$$

where:

W^P = Portfolio asset weight

W^B = Benchmark asset weight

R^P = Portfolio asset return

R^B = Benchmark asset return

R^{BT} = Benchmark total return

$\text{PMC} = \text{Portfolio market contribution} = \Sigma\ W^P/100 \times (1 + R^B /100)$

This analysis ignores the effects of currency, or rather, includes the effects of currency in both policy and selection. Consider the following simple example:

Investment category	Portfolio		Benchmark	
	% weight	% TWR	% weight	% TWR
US equities	60	4.0	75	5.9
German equities	15	12.6	10	10.8
Japanese equities	25	28.0	15	17
Total assets		11.3		8.1

All returns in sterling.

The relative return is the ratio of the portfolio's return to the benchmark's return:

$$\left(\frac{1.113}{1.081} - 1\right) \times 100 = 2.9\%$$

Looking at US equities:

$$\text{Policy} = (0.60 - 0.75) \times \left(\frac{1.059}{1.081} - 1\right) \times 100 = 0.3$$

The calculated policy number shows that US equities, as an asset, performed below that of the total benchmark i.e. US under-performed the benchmark (5.9% vs 8.1%) and therefore was a below average asset to be invested in. However, the fact that the portfolio was underweight (60 vs 75) in US equities was beneficial and therefore contributed positively to the relative return.

Moving on to the selection calculation, firstly define the total market contribution (PMC), which is sometimes known as a buy and hold return. This calculates the contribution of taking the portfolio's asset mix and applying benchmark returns. This effect needs to be stripped out before the selection contribution is calculated.

$$PMC = (.60 \times 1.059 + .15 \times 1.108 + .25 \times 1.17) = 1.0941$$

$$Selection = (0.60/PMC) \times (1.04 - 1.059) \times 100 = -1.0$$

The selection contribution is showing that the portfolio under-performed in US equities (4.0% vs 5.9%) and therefore contributed negatively towards the relative return.

The above analysis does not fully disaggregate the relative return and a residual is left which is normally explained away as the effects of the timing of changes to the asset mix of the portfolio over the period being analysed. One technique used to reduce the size of the residual is to undertake the calculations on a monthly basis using average capital employed for the asset weights, convert the results into a multiplicative basis (developed by the WM Company and not discussed here) and chainlink the results.

The currency effect

As mentioned earlier, this analysis does not cater for the impact of currency movements in each of the asset classes. This simplistic analysis was therefore further developed explicitly to split out the effects of currency movements.

The principle behind this analysis assumes that the portfolio's return, in a master currency, in a single market, is made up of a local currency return and the exchange rate change over the period of the return. Furthermore, the local return can be split into a local market (index or benchmark) return and a selection element. Without going into the full mathematical proof of this type of analysis the contributions can be defined from the following terms:

W^P = Portfolio weight in asset i (in %)

W^B = Benchmark weight in asset i (in %)

C_i = Currency change associated with asset i vs master currency

C_S = Total currency change for the benchmark

C_P = Total currency change for the portfolio

R^{Bi} = Benchmark return in local terms in asset i

B_s = Benchmark total market contribution

R^P = Portfolio return in asset i

giving:

Relative currency contribution (comparing the currency contribution in an asset against the total currency contribution of the portfolio) is defined as:

$$\text{Relative weight} \times \frac{\text{Currency change of asset i}}{\text{Total currency change of benchmark}}$$

$$\left(W^P - W^B\right) \times \left[\frac{(1+C_i/100)}{(1+C_s/100)} - 1\right]$$

Relative market contribution in its simplest form could be defined as the relative weight × relative market contribution. However, since the currency element has already been measured, it is necessary to build this into the calculation. This is done by adjusting the weights by the currency movement. The full definition is:

Relative weight (adjusted for currency) × Relative local benchmark return

where:

$$\text{Relative adjusted weight} = \left(W^P - W^B\right) \times \left[\frac{(1+C_i/100)}{(1+C_s/100)}\right]$$

$$\text{Relative benchmark return} = \left[\frac{(1+R^{Bi}/100)}{(1+B_s/100)} - 1\right]$$

Stock selection contribution = Benchmark/currency adjusted portfolio weight × Relative selection in local terms

In a similar way to the markets contribution before calculating the stock contribution the effects of currency and markets (already accounted for) have to be built into the formula. Again this is done by adjusting the asset weight. The full definition is:

$$\begin{array}{c}\text{Portfolio weight (adjusted} \\ \text{for benchmark and currency)}\end{array} = \frac{W^P \times (1+C_i/100) \times \left(1+R^{Bi/100}\right)}{\Sigma W^P \times (1+C_i/100) \times \left(1+R^{Bi}/100\right)}$$

$$\text{Relative stock selection} = \left[\frac{(1+R^P/100)}{(1+R^{Bi}/100)} - 1\right]$$

Table 5.1 illustrates the calculation of relative currency, markets and stock selection contributions.

Table 5.1 Basic information

		Portfolio			Benchmark		
Category	% Currency Changes vs Master Currency (US Dollar)	% Weight	% TWR (Master Currency)	% TWR (Local Currency)	% Weight	% TWR (Master Currency)	% TWR (Local Currency)
USA	-	60	4.0	-	75	5.9	5.9
Germany	2.5	15	12.6	9.9	10	10.8	8.1
Japan	**8.8**	**25**	**28.0**	**17.6**	**15**	**17.0**	**7.6**
TOTAL RETURN			11.3			8.1	

The relative return is the ratio of the portfolio's return to the benchmarks return i.e.

$$\left[\frac{1.113}{1.081} - 1\right] \times 100 \text{ or } 2.9\%$$

Currency contributions for each of the categories, for both the portfolio and benchmark are calculated as follows:

Category weight × currency change, i.e.:

	Portfolio	Benchmark
USA	$0.60 \times 0.0 = 0.0$	$0.75 \times 0.0 = 0.0$
Germany	$0.15 \times 2.5 = 0.38$	$0.10 \times 2.5 = 0.25$
Japan	$0.25 \times 8.8 = 2.2$	$0.15 \times 8.8 = 1.32$
Total currency contribution	$= 2.6$	$= 1.6$

Relative currency contributions can now be calculated. Taking Japan as an example:

$$\frac{\text{Relative currency}}{\text{contribution}} = \frac{\text{Difference in category}}{\text{weights}} \times \frac{\text{Currency change of local currency (yen) vs master}}{\text{currency (US dollar), relative to total benchmark currency contribution}}$$

$$(0.25 - 0.15) \times \left(\frac{1.088}{1.016} - 1\right) \times 100$$

$$= 0.7$$

Market contributions for each of the categories is calculated as follows:

$$\frac{\text{Category weight} \times \text{Currency change}}{\text{Total currency contribution}} \times \text{Local benchmark return}$$

	Portfolio	Benchmark
USA	$\left(\dfrac{0.60 \times 1.0}{1.0275}\right) \times 5.9 = 3.5$	$\left(\dfrac{0.75 \times 1.0}{1.0157}\right) \times 5.9 = 4.4$
Germany	$\left(\dfrac{0.15 \times 1.025}{1.02575}\right) \times 8.1 = 1.2$	$\left(\dfrac{0.10 \times 1.025}{1.0157}\right) \times 8.1 = 0.8$
Japan	$\left(\dfrac{0.25 \times 1.088}{1.02575}\right) \times 7.6 = 2.0$	$\left(\dfrac{0.15 \times 1.088}{1.0157}\right) \times 7.6 = 1.2$

Total currency contribution = 6.7   = 6.4

Relative market contributions can now be calculated. Again taking Japan as an example:

$$\text{Relative currency adjusted category weight} = (0.25 - 0.15) \times \left(\frac{1.088}{1.016}\right) = 0.1$$

Note here that both the category and total currency change have been converted to multiplicative format.

The relative benchmark return is $\left(\dfrac{1.076}{1.064} - 1\right) \times 100 = 1.1$

Therefore the relative market contribution = 0.1 × 1.1 = 0.1

Stock selection can finally be calculated. Again using Japan as an example:

Benchmark/currency adjusted portfolio weight =

$$\frac{0.25 \times 1.088 \times 1.076}{1.02575 \times 1.0667} = 0.267$$

$$\text{Relative stock selection} = \frac{\text{Portfolio local return}}{\text{Benchmark local return}} = \left(\frac{1.176}{1.076} - 1\right) \times 100 = 9.3$$

Therefore the stock selection contribution = 0.267 × 9.3 = 2.5

Once all calculations have been completed a table for the portfolio can be produced (Table 5.2), where the total contributions are 'chain-linked' from the individual contributions. For example, in Japan:

1.007 (currency) × 1.001 (markets) × 1.025 (selection) = 1.033

As the table shows the total relative contribution is 2.9% which can be analysed in two ways:

1) By category (–0.7% from USA, 0.3% from Germany, 3.3% from Japan).

Table 5.2 Contributions to relative return

Category	Currency %	Markets %	Selection %	Weighted Contribution
USA	0.2	0.1	-1.0	-0.7
Germany	0.0	0.1	0.2	0.3
Japan	**0.7**	**0.1**	**2.5**	**3.3**
TOTAL	1.0	0.3	1.7	2.9

2) By currency (1.0%), markets (0.3%), selection (1.7%).

Note that there is a positive contribution from 'currency USA'.

The formula as defined above gives:

$$(0.60 - 0.75) \times \left(\frac{1.000}{1.016} - 1 \right) \times 100 = 0.2$$

– a positive contribution from being lightly exposed to a category whose currency return is 0% compared with a currency return for the benchmark of +1.6%.

Recent developments

The above methodology was developed and enhanced throughout the 1980s. During this time it has served the industry well and indeed to date continues to be an appropriate analysis for a large number of portfolios. However, in an ever changing investment world with the introduction of more complex and sophisticated instruments, this methodology does begin to fail, particularly in the areas of derivatives and the more frequent tendency for managers to hedge away some or all of the currency risks contained in their portfolios.

A simple example of this would be a manager investing in a S&P Index future – here the portfolio initially has no currency exposure to the US$ and over time the currency exposure is limited to the variation margin. Using the above analysis, the whole of the future exposure would be considered to be exposed to the US$ – there is a need to differentiate between the hedge weight and the actual weight. Also with the differing methods of managing portfolios e.g. splitting the asset allocation from the stock selection, the use of TAAs. Who is making the investment decisions and how can the effects of these decisions be measured?

Two significant papers were published in 1994 which set out frameworks for new approaches to multicurrency attribution; Ankrim and Hensel in the March/April issue of the *Financial Analysts Journal* and Karnosky and Singer funded by the Research Foundation of the Institute of Chartered Financial Analysts.

The Ankrim and Hensel paper describes the methodology used by Frank Russell, the method used is additive rather than the multiplicative method as used by WM. However the formulae are essentially the same although this analysis identifies five separate attribution effects. These are derived by further decomposing the currency and selection components defined earlier.

The total currency component is based upon the change in exchange rates over the period of analysis. The decomposition breaks this currency change into two components – the return due to the difference in local interest rates over the period and the currency surprise which is the change in exchange rates over and above that return generated by the interest rate differentials.

For example, if the term deposit rates over the analysis period are 5% in the UK but 7% in the US then, everything else being equal, putting money into the US dollar account would produce a 2% greater return than holding the money in sterling. In theory exchange rates should adjust for this so with no currency surprise all the exchange rate movement should be explained by the interest rate differential. Of course in practice forward exchange rates which are derived from current exchange rates and interest rate differentials are a notoriously poor predictor of future spot rates. The aim of the analysis is to identify whether the manager is systematically benefiting/losing from these 'guaranteed' interest rate differential returns or whether he is correctly timing 'surprise' movements in the currency.

In formulae terms the interest rate differential term, known as the forward premium effect, is:

(Portfolio weight – Benchmark weight) (Differential interest rate –

Total 'guaranteed' return)

The surprise effect or the currency management effect is

(Portfolio weight – benchmark weight) (Currency surprise – Total surprise return) +

(Forward contract adjustment)

The other decomposition performed by this analysis is to decompose the selection effect into an interaction effect and a residual selection effect. Most performance attribution systems calculate selection using the weight in a category of a fund times the return difference between the fund and the benchmark. This is normally perfectly adequate but theoretically this term also includes the effect of the fund having a different weight from the benchmark as well as having achieved a different return. This effect is known as the interaction effect because it is achieved by the interaction of the weight difference with the return difference. The reason this is not normally shown is that it is difficult to attribute correctly. It is however important if the decision on the weights is completely separate from the stock selection decision. For example when a separate asset allocator is used then it is not correct to attribute the effect of a different weight to selection, however it is also incorrect to attribute the return difference to the market's contribution so the best that can be done is to state the contribution without assigning to either of the parties.

Selection is therefore:

Benchmark weight × (Portfolio return – Benchmark return)

whilst interaction is:

(Portfolio weight – Benchmark weight) (Portfolio return – Benchmark return)

The research paper by Karnosky & Singer takes a slightly different approach to the attribution between currency and markets. It challenges the assumption that contributions from currency are provided solely by the change in exchange rates over a period. In their model the currency contribution includes the local cash return. The model assumes that the currency and market decision are totally separate so there is one decision to invest in a currency then another to invest in one of the asset classes denominated in that currency. Of course if a currency is bought in the normal manner then it will earn interest in a bank account. The analysis allows this interest earned to be credited to the currency decision. This is similar to the forward premium effect but instead of just the difference in interest rates being part of the currency effect the whole local cash return is used.

If currency is calculated in this manner then market contributions become the return premia over local cash. This is suggesting that a manager with a proportion of his assets in a foreign currency will hold these in short term deposits and only move them into bonds or equities if he feels that these markets will outperform cash. This is analogous to the CAPM in which investors add value to a 'risk-free' rate. (The local cash return is not risk free in this circumstance because of the exposure to changes in exchange rate.)

The currency component is therefore:

(Portfolio weight – Benchmark weight) (Currency change + Local cash return)

Whilst the market component is:

(Portfolio weight – Benchmark weight) (Local market return – Local cash return)

The actual research paper contains more detail on the calculations and these include details on handling hedging and any contributions arising from the portfolio achieving different local cash returns from the benchmark.

Overall this approach is suitable for any investment process in which the currency decision is taken separately from the market one. Whether most managers evaluate market decisions in terms of return premia over cash is open to debate, however. Other managers who pick stocks on a global basis will not find this analysis relevant to their investment process. In fact some of these managers will take issue with any of these attribution approaches as none of them will reflect their investment process.

The main effect of the analysis is to take a positive contribution out of markets and put it into currency. This may have the effect of changing the relative importance of the two contributions in the eyes of many people. The debate on the merits of this approach will be particularly contentious where remuneration is based upon contributions to return!

The two attribution approaches described above do require more data than the straightforward currency, markets and selection model. Both analyses require short term local interest rates in all countries which are straightforward to collect in most cases for standard months and quarters. However, when there are transactions within a period, and a rate is required to the end of the period, then the data collection issues begin to be more intractable.

Further issues to be considered

Even with a new intellectual framework for attribution we are left with the problems of new instruments and fund structures. The main problems to be addressed are stock index futures, tactical asset allocation/currency overlay management, options and risk.

The treatment of futures

There are a number of issues regarding how to account for derivatives particularly futures in the context of the performance of the portfolio. The fact that the futures contract is not a real asset means that it is viewed differently by different users. In theory the return calculation will suffice for the derivative category. However, the problem lies in what data is being analysed. Are we looking at only the variation margin or should we be trying to look at the full economic exposure? This also has a knock on effect when trying to analyse the attribution, as was hinted at earlier.

Various work has been undertaken in this area, in particular LIFFE, for the UK market, published their 'industry standard' approach to UK futures. Its main findings are summarised below:

- It is not possible to measure performance on a 'margin payment' i.e. by using the capital gain on the futures position against either that of the equity or the cash components of the portfolio. This would lead ultimately to nonsensical figures for the return on parts of the portfolio. The main element of the return on the futures position has been its exposure to the underlying assets.

- The overall asset class return is produced by combining the return on both the real and synthetic assets.

- The investment income on the cash backing the futures contract should be transferred between the cash sector and the underlying asset class.

Unfortunately, this did not tackle the issues arising from futures being taken out in currencies outside that of the domicile of the portfolio.

The other reality is that some accounting systems are incapable of providing the required data and a lot of portfolios are forced to report only on the variation margin.

The main point from a performance point of view is not the return on the derivative *per se* – this is often fairly meaningless, it is to identify if the derivative has added or lost value to the portfolio. To this extent most reports follow the approach of showing performance including and excluding the derivatives. This can be done at the total portfolio level or at an individual asset class e.g. UK equities (inc and ex derivatives).

One standard approach, as defined by The WM Company, used in the treatment of futures is as follows:

- Classify the futures as an individual category grouped with the underlying asset e.g.

  UK equities   (Total)
  UK   (Category)
  FTSE 100 Futures (Category)

- A separate cash commitment category is also required for each committed currency, in the above sample sterling, i.e.

  Cash/Other
  Cash   (Total)
  UK cash commitment   (Category)

- The future is shown based on full economic exposure with equal and opposite entries against the futures lines and the cash commitment line.

- To avoid unnecessary complications with exchange rates, both the future and the cash commitment should be processed in local currency.

- The value of the future is simply = Future price × Unit of trading × No. of contracts.

- No investment income is received on a futures position and therefore income should be allocated to the synthetic futures position from the cash commitment. That is:

  - for a long position, futures income will be positive and cash commitment income will be negative;

  - for a short position, futures income will be negative and cash commitment income will be positive;

  - in both cases the entries will be equal and opposite.

- At each valuation date a purchase/sale entry is required to adjust the cash commitment by the amount of the variation margin. This ensures that the cash commitment still covers the full exposure, and cash is set aside to cover the variation margin. The futures category will show a gain/loss of this amount.

An example of this is covered below and has been derived from an example in the LIFFE document.

Asset class	Market value, £	Capital gain, £	Income, £	Return, %
UK equities	17800	872	214	6.1
Real asset	16000	800	160	6.0
Future	1800	72	54	7.0
Cash	2200	66	3	
Actual cash	4400	120	3	
Cash commitment	−1800	−54	3	

But while this methodology is acceptable in the UK other markets have difficulty with this approach. Appendix 3 is an extract from a paper[1] on the subject from a South African perspective. Arriving at an agreed international standard is not easy – a subject which we discuss more fully in Chapter 7.

TAA and currency overlays

The problem with tactical asset allocation and currency overlay management lies in the calculation of the selection contribution. The traditional attribution system

---

[1] 'Measuring the Impact of Futures & Options on Investment Portfolios; A South African Perspective'. Adrian C Ryder & Heather D McLeod: Presented to the Annual Convention of the Actuarial Society of South Africa, November 1992.

by default assigns the cross term arising from a combination of different weights and different returns to the selection contribution as described earlier. This is acceptable when asset allocation and stock selection is being handled by the same manager. If these are separate functions then the selection skills of the manager, who is actually picking the stocks, will not be correctly analysed. Identifying the cross term is simple but analysing it is less straightforward. All that may be possible is to state what it is and allow the reader to interpret it as required. Even so the costs incurred in switching assets between markets are borne by the local market portfolio, if actual stocks are traded to achieve the change, and this can depress the relative return of the portfolio.

Options and risk

The issue with options and risk is how to give credit in an attribution system for an outcome that was avoided. If we only concentrate on the return then the cost of unexercised options will simply be a drag on performance. The difficulty is in valuing the fact that the owner slept easier in bed knowing that he had this protection.

Conclusion

The ideal requirement is a flexible methodology which can be adjusted to meet the different management styles available, the ever increasing set of complex investment instruments, as well as the audience the analysis is aimed at. This could be achieved by defining a set of basic building blocks (contribution types) which can be combined in different ways to meet the needs of the analyser. Another important factor is to have a methodology which is practical to implement given the data sets available from investment accounting systems – accounting systems do not normally hold the reasons why managers make investment decisions!

The above attribution analysis is commonly used to analyse global portfolios where equities have been broken down by country and bonds by currency. There are many other types of attribution. Bond attribution (particularly popular in the US and Europe) typically breaks down returns into the following contributions, time (return due to passage of time), term structure change, sector, rating, maturity dependence and specific bond characteristics. Other types of equity attribution include the decomposition of the return into risk, manager style, sector, security, and a buy and hold contribution. Again, this method is very popular in the US.

However, no matter what attribution analysis is used the key question to consider is – Who is the attribution analysis for, the manager to analyse his decisions or the owner of the money to see how well the manager is performing?

Clearly each has different levels of understanding of the investment world and too sophisticated an attribution analysis may be wasted on the lay pension fund trustee.

The issues

The use of detailed data with complex formulae may give an air of accuracy to the data which is unjustified in practice. As we discuss in the next chapter much of the data is of questionable accuracy and over-refining the analysis of such data is pointless.

A further concern is that the search for simplified numbers to represent portfolio performance conceals the true complexity of the process. The numerical analysis still requires considerable qualitative judgement and careful interpretation. Moreover the analysis has to bear some relationship to the management structure and the decision making process.

It is also argued that the techniques being applied to analysis are ahead of the development of agreed standards for the industry. Not only are we a long way from agreement on specific investment data but the handling and reporting of such data through the legal and accounting professions can be very variable.

Some of these issues will be examined in the following chapters.

Practicalities of data collection

Introduction

As we have seen in looking at performance measurement, we require information for both sides of the equation in order to carry out the task. We need data on the benchmark in order to establish the performance standard and we need data on the fund which is to be measured.

In this chapter we examine the problems of collecting the required data and the pitfalls which may be encountered are examined. We begin by looking at the data associated with the benchmarks, since many of the problems encountered in this area will be common to the fund also.

We then look at those problems which are fund specific. Where the benchmark is a universe of funds, however, the problems at the fund level can feed back into the benchmark.

Benchmark data: prices

The basic building brick for all performance measurement is the asset price, whether the asset be equity shares, bonds, property or gold bars. For those assets which are frequently traded and quoted on an active exchange, such as equity shares in a large company, there should be no problem in establishing a price. But what is a price? Is it the contract price of the last bargain recorded in those shares? Is it the market makers quoted price at a specified time and place? In which case is it the bid or the offer price? It can be seen that even for, what should be, the simplest case there are complications. We will look at each of the major asset classes and the problems associated with establishing prices at a specified date, say 31 December.

Equity share prices

For most equity shares which are quoted, there is a recognised official market in those shares. This is usually the prime source of data on the shares but there are various levels of data, depending on the type of market trading.

Where continuous trading between market makers and brokers exists market makers quotes are available. These quotes may be collected such that the highest bid price and the lowest offer price can be established in order to achieve the narrowest spread of prices. Depending on the ultimate requirement either the bid or offer price can be used or the mid-price between the two. This last is the most commonly used price for valuation and index construction uses.

The next problem is the time of day that the price is collected. Traditionally a 'closing' price was used, i.e. the price quoted at the time the exchange closed. With modern-day electronic trading away from a physical exchange trading floor it is difficult to establish when the exchange has closed. To overcome this problem a specified time is usually set to mark the 'official close of trading'. In most of the developed exchanges this practice is further enhanced by the publication of official 'close of trading' prices for all the shares quoted on the exchange. This practice is also common even where the trading mechanism is different; for example where an open outcry auction takes place to establish the share trading price.

Thus for the great majority of shares there will be an official closing price from an official exchange source. The key characteristic of this price is that it is widely accepted as THE PRICE of the share for valuation purposes regardless of the quantity of shares being valued.

Thus in the UK the guidelines for investment manager reporting published by the Pensions Research Accounting Group (PRAG) recommended 'that prices be the recognised official closing prices in each market on the last UK week day of the reporting period. In order of preference, price types should be market mid, last trade, other single price'.

Since it would be impractical for all users requiring prices to approach the various exchanges for closing prices it is accepted practice that specialised agencies do so and disseminate the information. Thus such organisations as Reuters, Extel, Telstat, Telekurs, etc, carry out this function and most users thus acquire their price data at one remove from the original source. The main problem with this process is the accuracy with which the raw data is collected, collated, transposed to electronic format and transmitted. Cross checking mechanisms can identify most errors but they can still arise and distort the final product, be that a portfolio valuation or an index.

For the less developed markets official closing prices are not always available and direct contact with the traders may be necessary. If the different collecting agencies use different sources at slightly different times of the day the result may be several 'official' closing prices for the same share! The various producers of benchmarks (indices) may therefore produce slightly different results as a result of price variations at source.

A real life experience will illustrate the problem. Fund A used three separate organisations X, Y and Z, from which it received valuation and performance data. Z consistently produced valuations different from X and Y and was dropped because they were regarded as having produced 'faulty' valuations.

It transpired on investigation that X and Y both used the same data provider while Z used a different source. The prices over which they differed were for more obscure, less frequently traded, securities, prices for which Z approached the market makers directly for an up to date price. Data provided to X and Y by their source was less up to date and, by most standards, less accurate as an indicator of current value. Yet because Z was the 'odd man out' his prices and hence valuations were deemed to be faulty!

Bond prices

For many bonds, particularly where they are government, or government agency, bonds quoted on an official exchange, the source and practice of collecting prices is similar to that for equities. Many bond benchmarks include bonds which do not fall into this category, however, and establishing prices can be more complicated. The bulk of bond trades are 'over the counter' and trade prices are more jealously guarded. The price collecting agencies use different traders as their pricing source and thus pricing differences can occur across benchmarks, particularly if they are not using a common 'indicative' bargain size.

A further complication can arise if the price collectors do not properly differentiate between 'clean' and 'dirty' prices. The former are prices excluding any interest accrued on the bond and interest is accounted for separately as part of income. 'Dirty' prices are total prices including any adjustment for interest. Many errors can arise from careless handling of these prices.

Property/real estate prices

Since trading in properties is infrequent and each property is, in any case, unique, the pricing of property assets presents an even greater problem. Consequently there are fewer benchmarks in this area and those that exist tend to rely on either traded prices of a cross section of properties over a recent defined period or on values estimations of a sample of properties at a specified date. The margin for variations in benchmarks is therefore considerably wider than for quoted shares and bonds.

Commodities, collectables and other prices

The pricing of other assets span the spectrum of problems encountered with the assets already covered. At one level the commodity may be frequently traded on a recognised official market (such as the London bullion market for gold) in which case an official closing price is available, as for equities, and the market performance is itself the benchmark. At the other extreme, fine art or antiques are infrequently traded and few benchmarks are available. Those that are utilise methods similar to property and are subject to similar, or more extreme, variances due to subjective valuation estimates. In practice the use of benchmarks for asset specific management performance purposes is not common in these areas, however, and returns are usually judged against other assets such as equities or bonds.

Benchmark data: exchange rates

In some ways exchange rates can be looked at as just another asset price – the price of currency – where the asset is the currency. For practical purposes, however, currency affects all the other assets if they are outside the base country and exchange rates add an extra complication to benchmarks and portfolio valuations which have an international dimension.

The markets in currencies are totally 'over the counter', that is they are conducted directly between principals over the telephone or other electronic media. Moreover it is a twenty-four hour market so that there is no 'official close' and no single time zone which is taken as a universal base.

This clearly offers scope for considerable variation in pricing even when the base market price for the asset can be established. Thus two producers of international equity indices may have identical local market prices but one uses London prices at 16:00 Hs GMT and the other New York prices at 16:00 Hs EST. The dollar or sterling price for the asset incorporated into the benchmark/index will almost certainly be different and, during volatile currency market conditions, significantly so.

Moreover even if the rates were both taken in London, using different traders as the source can lead to variations, albeit less significant, in the exchange rates gathered. More recently steps have been taken to overcome this problem by establishing a commonly accepted single source of exchange rates, distributed through the Reuters network, in the form of the WM/Reuters Closing Spot Rates based on London quotes taken at 16:00 Hs. This is now the source of exchange rates recommended by PRAG within the UK.

Benchmark data: company data

For equity benchmarks, data other than prices may be necessary. The most commonly accepted form of index used for performance measurement is the capitalisation weighted index. Furthermore the need to measure total return, rather than just capital movement, requires information on income or dividends.

Issued capitals

For capitalisations of constituent companies in an index to be calculated, up-to-date information on the issued capital of the companies is required. In the developed stock exchanges, companies are required to register changes in issued capital when they occur. In practice, delays often occur both in registration and in subsequent dissemination of this information into the public domain. Establishing accurate information on issued capital is, therefore, a major problem for index compilers and variations can, and often do, appear across different indices.

For the less developed markets the problems are compounded, with the standards of reporting at both the company and stock exchange levels much less reliable. In some markets legal constraints exist on foreign ownership and index compilers also differ on the treatment of such issues. Similarly some compilers limit the capitalisation of companies to an estimate of the 'free float', that is the proportion of shares available for trading in the market and not held by other agencies or long term holders.

These issues are unlikely to be a problem for the compiler of the index but a proper understanding of them is necessary if the users of the index are not to be confused or misled by the data they collect in the form of the index.

Dividends

For the developed markets this presents few problems insofar as the information is usually available in a timely fashion through the official exchanges. The problems are more prevalent in the developing markets where information on dividend declarations, the timing of payments and the pricing of securities ex-dividend may be less disciplined.

These problems for the compilers of benchmarks are compounded for the users, because of the different practices adopted by different compilers. Variations in the algorithms used can lead to variations in calculated returns so that a full understanding is necessary if confusion is to be avoided.

For the index or benchmark compilers the problems are, therefore, a combination of practical availability of data, the reliability of the collecting process and the acceptability of the data as a standard or benchmark. For the valuation of the individual funds these problems also exist but there are some extra practical difficulties to be overcome.

Fund data: prices

Although compilers of benchmarks have considerable data problems, as described above, they usually confine the constituents of their benchmarks or indices to assets on which data is, at least, more readily available. At the fund level the performance measurer has a much broader universe of assets with which to contend. We will examine the problems associated with specific assets which can arise, over and above the more general problems already discussed.

For the fund valuer, or performance measurer, a further general problem exists which is common to all assets. This is the basic problem of accurately transferring the data when collected into the valuation system. The process of handling many items of, seemingly, mundane information still involves human intervention and the scope for error is considerable. Minimising these errors and establishing systems for recognising and correcting them presents a major problem.

Most of the problems at fund level occur in the area of prices. In general the holdings of the fund can be established with accuracy. Errors can still occur, particularly when capitalisation changes take place in equities and in the area of cash balances.

Equity share prices

In addition to the general problems already covered, the fund is faced with difficulties in pricing the less commonly traded equities. In cases where the shares are traded on a recognised exchange a price is available through the official exchange channels but it may be a poor indication of current value if trades have not taken place for some time. For shares which are unquoted the price used can be the book or cost price or an indicative price based on the latest transaction, if any, in the shares. Gathering such data can be a time and cost consuming exercise, while the result is more likely to distort the performance measurement process than to enhance it. At best, therefore, the valuation of the equity portfolio is an approximation of current worth. The nature and size of the portfolio will determine how close an approximation it is.

In addition to the actual price, the classification of the share can present practical difficulties. This can arise either because the shares are quoted on more than one exchange or because different index providers classify the company in a different industrial sector. These problems are less relevant at the total fund valuation and performance level since the asset will be included somewhere. When more detailed performance analysis is carried out, for example attribution analysis, complications can arise. A few examples will illustrate the problems.

Example 1
Hong Kong and Shanghai Bank (HSBC) was for a long time quoted in Hong Kong and regarded as an overseas asset by most UK investors. When it acquired

Midland Bank large numbers of shares were issued in exchange and a UK quote obtained. The company was included in the FT–SE–A index series as a major constituent. Some funds subsequently recorded all their HSBC shares as part of their UK portfolio including both shares already held and those newly acquired as a result of holding Midland Bank. Other funds recorded newly acquired shares as part of their UK portfolio while retaining existing holdings as part of their Hong Kong portfolio. Yet other funds regarded the whole of their holding as part of their Hong Kong portfolio.

Example 2

Royal Dutch and Shell Transport & Trading as well as Unilever NV and Unilever Ltd are often regarded as alternate ways of investing in the same company. Prices of the separate parts, although generally following the same trend, can move apart sufficiently to generate arbitrage trading. Where the shares are classified within the portfolio and whether gains or losses are part of a UK or Dutch portfolio at any time can present problems for the performance measurer.

Example 3

A UK Investment Trust, wholly invested in Japan, is held as part of a UK equity portfolio by one fund and as part of a Japanese portfolio in another fund. In its recommendations PRAG at least suggests that such situations are substantiated in notes to the valuations but individual funds may still choose where to classify the stock and thus influence performance differently from fund to fund and from fund to benchmark.

Bond prices

Where bonds are held there is a high probability that some of them will be infrequently traded. In some countries non-traded bonds are often held. Official prices are not available for such instruments and pricing for valuation and performance measurement must rely on specialist agencies.

The most common practice is for bond prices to be established through a matrix pricing mechanism. Effectively the characteristics of the bond such as maturity date, coupon, credit rating, liquidity, etc, are assessed. Bonds with closely similar characteristics are grouped together into a box or cell and a quoted bond with similar characteristics is used as a pricing guide.

The accuracy of such price estimates depends upon the complexity and reliability of the algorithm and how closely the characteristics of the bond can be matched. Furthermore the absence of official prices means that different pricing sources may be used by different pricing agencies, adding further to the scope for discrepancies.

Fund data: income

For the compilers of indices income is always a notional factor, they do not have to collect it physically, merely to assume it is collected at a specified time after its declaration. For the fund and the performance measurer income presents a very real practical problem.

In many cases the receipt of the income may differ in timing from that assumed by the index or benchmark compiler and can thus affect performance. In other cases the income is not received at all. This may be due to withholding tax complications and the ability to recover the tax varying from fund to fund. Or it may simply be lost through administrative incompetence. Either way it can influence calculated returns and performance relative to a benchmark.

Fund data: derivatives

These pose a separate problem for the performance measurer at the fund level. Most derivatives, options and futures, are traded on official exchanges and a current price is available. Some, however, are customised over the counter transactions and valuation can present a problem.

But the current price of the derivative instrument is not the key problem for the valuer and performance measurer. The complexities of these problems are addressed in more detail in Chapter 7. In terms of data collection the problems relate to the need for clear definitions in the accounting process so that the assets concerned (the underlying asset, the derivative, cash on margin, etc) can be identified and properly allocated. This calls for considerable co-operation between the fund manager or custodian and the valuer or performance measurer.

This is a further area which highlights the need for standards of treatment, a subject which is examined in Chapter 7. Given the difficulties of establishing a 'true' price and hence a 'true' value it is important to agree an acceptable standard so that, at least, exercises in performance measurement can be carried out on a comparable basis. This applies not only to the investment community but also to the associated disciplines such as accountancy and law.

The issues

A major issue for practitioners is clearly one concerning the reliability of the end product. As has been illustrated the price of an asset is, at best, an approximation. Any variances such approximations produce relative to a 'true' value will be compounded by data error in the collection and calculation processes. Variations in algorithms will also introduce differences between benchmark compilers and between performance measurers. Any valuation and performance figure should, therefore, be accompanied by an indication of its accuracy (x or y% plus or minus an error factor). This might prevent the many misunderstandings and disputes which arise when index numbers or performance returns show minor variations between compilers or measurers.

It should also make practitioners particularly wary of using the figures for performance related fees which depend upon minimal variances from the benchmark.

Over the longer term most of these data errors will smooth out and the long term return calculations are likely to provide a reasonably accurate estimate of the actual performance of the fund. Only if there is a systematic error, in an algorithm for example, will there be serious risk that the performance measurement process is misleading.

Performance standards

Introduction

Standards relating to performance measurement can be considered in two categories: technical and commercial. In the area of technical standards fall such items as basic formula, for example the calculation of a time weighted return, or basic data, for example a share price or an exchange rate to be used in the calculations. In the area of commercial standards fall such items as the claims to historic performance which an organisation can make in promoting its products or services. In this chapter these areas are examined separately and the evolution of standards to the present day in the major markets is discussed.

Technical standards

In Chapter 1 the evolution of performance measurement was described and it is clear that concern about the establishment of correct methodologies in calculating performance was present at the very beginning. Thus the BAI report emphasised the need to calculate TWRs on a consistent basis when examining different funds. Similarly the IIMR in its report offered a methodology for calculating a TWR *'using a comparatively simple approximation which it is believed will normally be accurate enough for most purposes'*.

In those early days it was recognised that the calculations would often be constrained by availability of data and the 'approximation' could cover a range of possible outcomes. It was not felt necessary, or desirable, to be too specific in defining the methodology. As a result, different methodologies were adopted by performance measurers while all adhered to the basic necessity to calculate a TWR as well as a MWR.

Effectively the timing of cash flows could vary depending on the frequency of calculation or the assumptions made in the timing within the sub-period (e.g. whether to assume cash ̇. ws at the start, middle or end of the period). Similarly while all accepted the principle that large cash flows should be day-dated, or pro-rated within the period, there was no standard established as to what constituted 'large'. Some measurers define it as 5% of initial asset value, others might define it as 10%.

Developments in North America

In establishing its 'performance standards' for the US market, the AIMR suggested that portfolios should be valued at least quarterly but monthly valuation and geometric linking is preferred. Portfolios should be revalued where a cash flow exceeds 10% of portfolio assets. In defining total return AIMR recommended that returns should include income and capital appreciation based on market values but no detailed recommendations were made as to the timing of receipts of income including the knotty problem of withholding taxes on overseas dividends and interest. Accounting on an accruals basis was recommended.

Thus minimum standards were recommended but not definitive standards. Consequently variations can still exist where measurers comply with the minimum but impose their own, more stringent, standards, or other variations within the minimum.

Nevertheless the establishment of a set of minimum standards has brought the subject to the fore and the AIMR in the USA and the Pension Investment Association of Canada (PIAC) in Canada have laid down minimum standards for the calculation, presentation and use of performance data. Much of their concern, however, lies in the area of the presentation and use with particular emphasis on the need to present a clear, accurate and fair presentation of investment performance so that prospective purchasers of investment management services are not misled. This aspect is covered later in the chapter.

The AIMR standards relating to technical issues are summarised below but, as already mentioned, they do not attempt to specify details of calculation or the algorithms to be used, although best practice examples are put forward for adoption.

- Returns are time-weighted to minimise the effect of contributions/withdrawals – various methods are acceptable.

- Returns must be total i.e. include capital growth and income.

- Calculations must be performed at least quarterly, but monthly is preferred.

- Calculations must be based on trade-dated accounting.

- Income/interest must be treated on an accrual basis.

- Portfolios should be revalued after major cash flows (greater than 10% of the portfolio's market value).

- Long term results must be compound annualised, not averages.

- Results for any one asset class (e.g. an equity portfolio) should include all cash equivalents and securities used in place of the asset class.

Evolution in the UK

In the UK and Europe, and to some extent in the area of international portfolios, the various performance measurement organisations aimed to follow best practice within the limitations of data availability.

In the UK, in particular, the measurement of pension fund performance was dominated from early days by the two organisations – CAPS and The WM Company. General methodologies recommended by organisations such as the IIMR or the National Association of Pension Funds (NAPF) were readily accepted. Indeed the two organisations had a significant input into the establishment of such recommendations.

Nevertheless CAPS and The WM Company adopted slightly different algorithms, especially in the treatment of cash flows and investment income. These differences reached a climax in 1992 when their estimate of the returns achieved on UK equities by UK pension funds differed by over 1%.

A detailed analysis carried out by the two organisations sought to identify the source of such differences. Some 0.95% of the 1.1% total difference was found to be attributable to variations in the mix of institutions within their respective samples (0.70%) and in the sample of portfolios within institutions (0.25%). Only 0.15% could be attributed to technical factors such as the allowance by CAPS for dealing costs on the investment of new money.

The two organisations also differed in their calculation of total return on the benchmark index – the FT–SE–Actuaries All Share Index. This difference stemmed from the different treatment of dividend income with The WM Company assuming income is received and reinvested on the XD date while CAPS assumed a delay in the receipt and hence reinvestment of the income. This difference was resolved when the FT–A began to produce its own total return indices, assuming reinvestment on the XD date, and thus effectively establishing the standard.

Despite the minor differences which have occurred between the two organisations it is, probably, fair to say that they have pioneered the standards in performance measurement and presentation in the UK. The existence of two such dominant organisations and their close and continuing contact with the professional bodies such as the IIMR, NAPF and the Faculty and Institute of Actuaries has meant that best practice has been relatively easy to implement. Consequently the professional bodies have felt less need to promulgate their own definition of standards.

Recent developments, with the complexities of derivative instruments and attribution analysis as examples, have raised the issue to the fore once again. The publication of the AIMR standards has also made the European organisations reconsider the necessity of formalising their own position. A good example of such co-operation within the area of technical standards has been in the area of exchange rates. In Chapter 6 we touched on the problems of establishing a common exchange rate given the different sources and the time zones of operation of the various performance measurers. These problems were largely overcome when, after substantial discussion and negotiation among interested parties a standard was established in the form of the WM/Reuters series of exchange rates. Such an example indicates how technical standards can be established but there are many other areas involving the pricing and classification of securities where similar co-operation is needed.

Broadly speaking the technical standards are relevant to the users of performance measurement services to help in the understanding of the returns and to facilitate proper analysis and interpretation. The ultimate aim of technical standards is to establish a common basis for the classification and valuation of securities, assets, portfolios and funds and a proper treatment of their cash flows. This in turn will promote the effective construction, selection and use of samples and benchmarks for the measurement and evaluation of investment performance.

In principle there should be little to prevent these standards being established internationally. More difficulty is likely to be met in the area of commercial standards.

Commercial standards

The need for commercial standards as opposed to technical standards stems from the practice of organisations offering fund management services, of whatever kind, laying claim to particular levels of past performance. In Chapter 4 we touched on the basic tenets to be observed when using performance measurement to assess fund managers. As much as anything it was the need to assess the claims of fund managers more effectively that prompted the evolution of disciplined performance measurement. It is perhaps surprising therefore that it has taken some thirty years for a formalisation of standards to evolve although informal standards have been accepted to varying degrees in different markets.

The AIMR standards in the USA

For a single fund there are few problems in this area provided best practice in the area of technical standards has been observed. A large part of the AIMR standards is aimed at the problem of presenting composite data. This is not surprising since the current AIMR standards introduced in 1993 evolved from the original work of the Financial Analysts Federation (FAF) Committee for Performance Presentation Standards first published in 1987. This committee was formed as a result of concern over the presentation of performance records to the public and the possible misuse and abuse of performance figures in advertising and promotional material.

The AIMR requirements with respect to the presentation of composite results are summarised below.

A Construction of composites

- All actual, fee-paying, discretionary portfolios must be included in at least one composite.

- No linkage of simulated or model portfolios with actual portfolios is allowed.

- Non-fee paying portfolios may be included provided such inclusion is disclosed.

- If investment restrictions inhibit the application of an intended investment strategy the portfolio may be excluded.

- Portfolio returns should be asset weighted within the composite using beginning of period weightings.

- New portfolios must not be added to a composite until the start of the next performance period.

- Portfolios no longer under management must be included in historical composites for the periods they were under management.

- Portfolios must not be switched from one composite to another unless client guidelines have changed enough to justify it.

- Changes in an organisation must not lead to altering composite results.

- Convertibles and other hybrid instruments should be treated consistently.

B Presentation of composites

- At least a 10 year record (or since inception if shorter) must be presented.

- Retroactive compliance is recommended but not required.

- For any period for which compliance is claimed annual returns for all years is required. Annualised cumulative performance is recommended.

- Proportions of taxable and non-taxable securities should be disclosed.

- Internal and external dispersions of returns should be shown.

- Presentation of supplemental information is recommended when deemed to be valuable.

C Disclosures

- For each time period the number of portfolios, total assets and percent of assets of firm's total must be disclosed.

- Segments of multi-asset or balanced portfolios included in single asset composites must be disclosed and allocation of cash included.

- Disclosure of whether results are gross or net of fees and a schedule of fees must be presented.

- Existence of a minimum asset size below which portfolios are excluded from a composite must be disclosed.

- If settlement date rather than the preferred trade date accounting is used it must be disclosed.

- Use and extent of leverage must be presented.

- Inclusion of non-fee paying portfolios should be disclosed.

The standards were aimed, primarily, at portfolios of US securities but other assets such as international securities, real estate and private investment were incorporated into the general guidelines. An important aspect of the AIMR standards is that independent verification is required. It was recognised that presentation practices vary throughout the world.

The NAPF standards in the UK

In the UK the best practice with respect to the technical standards, as already indicated, were well within the guidelines. As with AIMR, however, some leeway was allowed in specific technical issues although the measurers were encouraged to agree uniform methodologies. In the area of commercial, or presentational standards, the environment was different.

The NAPF established two levels of compliance in its 'Voluntary Code of Practice for Advertising Investment Managers' Performance Records' published in January 1992. This was designed for 'Balanced Discretionary UK Pension Funds' but its principles could be applicable to specialist funds, themselves the subject of a subsequent report in 1995.

Level One representation included all balance funds under management. Level Two included EITHER the largest proportion under a single monitoring regime OR, if multiple regimes are aggregated, the aggregation must be verified by an independent monitor.

The number and value of funds managed and the number and value of funds included in the measured returns must be stated.

Further qualifications were included:

- Total asset returns must be clearly identified as including or excluding property.

- The percentage of total funds represented by the largest fund must be stated to be more or less than 20% of the managers' discretionary portfolios.

- Measurer must be named.

- Comparisons should be like with like, e.g. weighted averages vs weighted averages not medians.

- If rolling returns are shown the full five year rolling return must be shown.

The emphasis on the measurer stems from the background to performance measurement in the UK. Pension funds in the NAPF were required to have their fund performance measured by an independent measurer. As already mentioned the UK has been dominated by two measurement organisations who are assumed to carry out due diligence in providing and endorsing aggregate returns for fund management organisations.

By contrast in the USA it has been estimated that only 12% of US firms[1] have results calculated by an independent measurer.

Other regions

Further constraints to applying AIMR standards exist in other markets, due partly to different accounting and reporting practices. In Japan, for example, the basic calculation for determining the rate of return is different. Securities are carried at book value and returns are expressed as realised gains as a percentage of book value. A 4% return on book cost is required.

In the Netherlands the Verzekeringskamer (Insurance Chamber) lay down a requirement that funds achieve a 4% yield or return. Any shortfall in any one

---

[1] Survey by The Spaulding Group Inc.

year must be made up by special levy. Bonds may be valued at book price while equities are to be valued at market price.

Whilst there is no prohibition on funds undertaking their own performance measurement according to their own standards these differing local requirements can be in conflict with best practice in the USA or UK and inhibit the widespread adoption of such standards as those recommended by the AIMR or the NAPF.

As the adoption of performance measurement becomes more widespread however the need to apply standards which are acceptable internationally will increase. At their 1994 Congress in Edinburgh the European Federation of Financial Analysts Societies (EFFAS) set up a committee to investigate the subject of standards and put forward proposals on a Europe wide basis.

The issues

The evolution of performance measurement over the past thirty years has brought a reasonable degree of standardisation in the technical areas despite the failure to formalise standards. Thus formulae for calculating MWR or TWR vary in only minor details. Little attention has been devoted to standardising basic data sources except in one or two areas however, and as discussed in Chapter 6 there are many practical difficulties once we move outside the area of securities of large companies or government bonds traded on recognised major exchanges. Is the pursuit of globally agreed standards worthwhile? For most funds their concern is to conform to their local market requirements and global standards may conflict with local practice.

In the area of commercial or presentational standards the local industry practices inevitably lead to local variations. Nevertheless the standards recommended by the AIMR and the NAPF have much in common and certainly have the same basic intention – to promote consistent and ethical representation of managers' investment results.

As funds and investment organisations become more international the need for global agreement increases but there will remain strong resistance by some of the world's markets, to 'cultural colonisation' from the Anglo-Saxon practices.

8

Risk

Introduction

The importance of the risk dimension in investment has been introduced earlier and has always been acknowledged in the industry. The whole concept of portfolio investment is based partly on the need to reduce risk by diversification.

The original BAI report on pension fund performance measurement concluded that fund performance should be measured in two dimensions – rate of return and risk. However, as already introduced in Chapter 3, the definition of risk for measurement purposes has posed major problems. Controversy surrounding the different approaches existed in the early days of performance measurement and still exists today.

The BAI report suggested the use of volatility or variability of returns as a risk measure, adopting the approach which had emerged from Markowitz et al in the previous decade. Thus the main thrust of developments in the USA, and in academic circles elsewhere, was based on this proxy for risk. Moreover, the calculation of volatility tended to be based on relatively short time periods and nominal returns.

The investor is well aware, however, that risk is a much more complex subject and his attitude to risk is very subjective. The insurance industry is well versed in all aspects of risk, including its multi-dimensional nature. Although risk is essentially a phenomenon with relevance to the future, it is commonly accepted that the past can provide useful guidance. Historic data can help in assessing probabilities of specific outcomes, but they have to be combined with aspects of costs, timeframes and liabilities.

It is no coincidence, therefore, that the perceptions of investment risk in the USA and UK diverged, the former rooted in the work of Markowitz and Modern

Portfolio Theory, the latter in the papers presented to the Institute and Faculty of Actuaries.

This chapter looks first at the early development of approaches to risk measurement emerging from MPT and subsequently how multidimensional approaches have evolved. Finally, there is an examination of the attitudes more prevalent in the UK.

Early development in the USA

As noted above, during the evolution of Modern Portfolio Theory in the 1950s, asset price volatility was selected as a convenient proxy for risk. A portfolio's 'total risk' could be measured by the standard deviation of returns over a number of periods. Therefore:

$$\text{Total risk} = S_p = \sqrt{\tfrac{1}{(N-1)}(\sum_{i=1}^{N} P_i^2 - N\overline{P}^2)}$$

where

S_p = Standard deviation of portfolio returns over N periods

P_i = Portfolio return for period $i = 1, \ldots, N$

$\overline{P}$ = Average return over N periods

Historic return variability gave an overall measure of the risks taken by an investment manager to achieve the portfolio return. For a given level of return, investors should prefer a return stream with lower variability. It could also be interpreted as a measure of diversification; the better diversified the portfolio, the lower the standard deviation of return.

In further work based on Sharpe's Capital Asset Pricing Model (CAPM), Treynor (1965) argued that return on equity portfolios was likely to be dominated by market factors and that the variability due to market movements could not be diversified away in a single market. He introduced the 'characteristic line', which was derived through simple linear regression of the portfolio's returns against those of an appropriate market index. This work was based on analysis of US Mutual Funds and so an appropriate market index was readily available. The technique allowed 'total' risk to be divided into what became known as:

Market risk
That part of the variability of return that is explained by general movements in the market. This was also known as 'non-diversifiable risk' or 'beta risk'.

Specific risk

The residual variability that is due to portfolio specific factors, also known as 'diversifiable risk' in that it would reduce to zero in a perfectly diversified or index portfolio.

In this single-factor model, the apportionment of the risk is based on the correlation coefficient, R_{pm}, between portfolio and market index returns:

$$R_{pm} = \frac{1}{(N-1) \times S_p \times S_m} (\sum_{i=1}^{N} P_i M_i - N\overline{PM})$$

where

M_i = Return on market index for period i, i = 1, . . . ,N

S_m = Standard deviation of market index returns over N periods

$\overline{M}$ = Average index return over N periods

From this we obtain

Market risk = $S_p \times R_{pm}$

Specific risk = $S_p \times \sqrt{(1 - R_{pm}^2)}$

and

$$(\text{Total risk})^2 = S_p^2 = (\text{Market risk})^2 + (\text{Specific risk})^2$$

Note that these measures are normally annualised to provide meaningful comparisons. Due to the compound nature of returns, this involves converting to and from logarithms to obtain correct annualised figures.

Related measures are:

R-squared (R^2)

The square of the correlation coefficient, R^2, represents the proportion of total variability that is explained by movements in the market index. This is a measure of diversification. The greater the R^2 relative to a market index, the lower the remaining opportunity to reduce variability further through diversification in the home market. Equally, a low R^2 for international returns relative to a 'home index' would indicate the diversification benefit of investing internationally.

Alpha (α)

This is the intercept of the characteristic line and measures whether the portfolio has achieved a systematically higher (or lower) return than the market index. This is a measure of differential return rather than risk and is a notoriously difficult parameter to estimate

Alpha = $\alpha_{pm} = \overline{P} - \beta_{pm} \times \overline{M}$

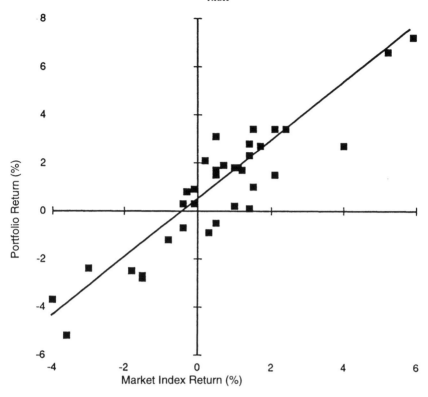

8.1 Characteristic line – portfolio v market index – monthly returns.

Beta (β)

The slope of the characteristic line, this represents the sensitivity of the portfolio's return to movements in the overall market. A beta greater than 1 for example means that the portfolio return would tend to fluctuate more than the underlying index and vice versa.

$$\text{Beta} = \beta_{pm} = R_{pm} \times \frac{S_p}{S_m}$$

An example of this linear regression to produce the characteristic line is shown in Fig. 8.1. This is based on 36 monthly returns for an equity portfolio against a market index (illustrative data only). In practice, the two principal single-factor measures of portfolio risk are beta and standard deviation (total variability). Beta is only a valid measure for single asset classes where there is an appropriate market index and a reasonably high correlation of returns. Otherwise figures will range from unreliable to meaningless. If total assets are being measured then standard deviation of returns is the only available measure.

Adoption of these risk measures in performance analysis has been fairly widespread in the USA. It was standard practice in the 1970s and 1980s to

	Time-Weighted Return (%)	Standard Deviation (%)	R² vs S&P 500	R² vs MSCI EAFE	Beta vs MSCI EAFE	Market Risk (%)	Specific Risk (%)
PORTFOLIO	4.8	18.3	0.25	0.92	0.76	17.5	5.3
MSCI EAFE	2.2	23.3	0.16	1.00	1.00	23.3	
S&P 500	11.4	13.7	1.00	0.16			
WM COMPOSITE	1.6	17.9	0.25	0.91	0.74	17.0	5.4
5th Percentile	5.3	21.0	0.28	0.94	0.85	19.8	8.8
Upper Quartile	3.4	19.5	0.25	0.92	0.80	18.5	7.7
Median	1.4	18.8	0.23	0.88	0.76	17.5	6.5
Lower Quartile	0.3	17.7	0.20	0.83	0.70	16.2	5.3
95th Percentile	-1.7	14.4	0.15	0.71	0.59	13.4	4.6

● E
□ S

8.2 Total portfolio performance – ranges of risk measures.

include analysis of total variability in performance reports, normally in the form of a scattergram of a universe of fund results plotting annualised return against annualised standard deviation of return. The individual fund result was plotted along with related market indices and sometimes a risk-free asset (e.g. 90-day T-Notes). This would be done at total assets level and sometimes repeated for individual countries and/or asset classes.

In many cases, beta and R-squared comparisons were also done, often showing rankings against a fund universe. As international investment grew in the 1980s, the same approach was adopted, using index benchmarks such as Morgan Stanley Capital International (MSCI) World or EAFE indices. R-squared relative to the S&P 500 index was often shown to measure the diversification benefit of international investment on the total fund.

An example of this kind of representation in performance reports is given by The WM Company's IMPACT service for the international assets of US and Canadian Pension Plans. This is shown in Fig. 8.2. In this example, the portfolio's monthly non-US equity returns have been compared with its benchmark, the MSCI EAFE Index. The annualised risk measures and their interpretation were as follows:

- Total variability was 18.3% and this subdivided into market risk at 17.5% and specific risk at 5.3%.

- R-squared against MSCI EAFE was 0.92, meaning that movements in the market index explained 92% of portfolio returns.

- Beta was less than 1 at 0.76 implying that the portfolio was invested in less volatile assets (markets or stocks) than the index as a whole.

- Finally R-squared for the portfolio against the domestic index, S&P 500, was fairly low at 0.25, implying that the international portfolio was reasonably effective in providing risk reduction to the total fund through diversification. However, over this period, the portfolio had a slightly higher correlation with the S&P 500 than the index, whose R-squared was lower at 0.16.

Risk-adjusted returns

Still based on this single-factor approach, Treynor and others went on to develop single measures of 'risk adjusted return' which sought to allow a fair comparison of the achievements of funds with different risk profiles. Four measures emerged, based on combinations of the following parameters:

- Whether beta or standard deviation is used as a proxy for risk

- Whether 'reward per unit of risk' or 'differential return' is measured

These measures all depend on the comparison of the portfolio return with a 'risk-free' rate of return and are outlined briefly below. For a fuller discussion of their relative merits, see Dietz and Kirschman (1990).[1]

1. 'Sharpe' measure = $(P_N - F_N)/S_p$

    where P_N = Portfolio return over N periods

    F_N = Risk-free return over N periods

    This measures the excess return achieved over the risk free rate for each unit of risk taken, with risk represented by the standard deviation of return.

2. 'Treynor' measure = $(P_N - F_N)/\beta_{pm}$

    This is identical to the Sharpe measure except that Beta is used as a proxy for risk.

3. Differential return measure = $P_N - \left\{ F_N + (M_N - F_N) \times \dfrac{S_p}{S_m} \right\}$

    where M_N = Market index return over N periods

    This measures the excess return over a benchmark portfolio with the same total risk as the portfolio concerned. This benchmark is obtained by combinations of the risk-free rate and the 'market portfolio' or index.

4. 'Jensen' Measure = $P_N - \left\{ F_N + (M_N - F_N) \times \beta_{pm} \right\}$

    Also known as 'Jensen's alpha', this is a variation on the differential return measure, but uses beta rather than standard deviation as a proxy for risk.

A key point is that those measures based on beta, namely the Treynor and Jensen measures, effectively ignore the unsystematic or specific risk element and so assume that the portfolio is perfectly diversified. The Sharpe measure does not make this assumption as it uses standard deviation as its proxy for risk. In addition, the Jensen measure, also know as Jensen's Alpha, is unique to a particular portfolio beta level. This means that it cannot be used to compare portfolios with different risk levels. Finally, all these measures are based on the CAPM and suffer from common problems relating to the model's underlying assumptions and its basis on historical returns.

---

[1] *Evaluating Portfolio Performance*, Peter O Dietz and Jeanette R Kirschman, Chapter 14 Managing investment portfolios, Warrent, Gorham & Lomont, 1990.

Table 8.1 InterPerf risk adjusted return schedule

MNGR: INT. MANAGER INC
ACCT: FUND NUMBER 1
Periods Ending June 1986

Non - U.S. Equity Universe

INTERPERF © 1990
INTERSEC RESEARCH CORP.

		Last Quarter		One Year		Two Years		Three Years		Four Years	
		U.S. $	LOCAL	U.S. $	LOCAL	U.S. $	LOCAL	U.S. $	LOCAL	U.S. $	LOCAL
TOTAL FUND RISK ADJ. RETURN RAR	HI	0.0		0.0		303.6		49.0 B		68.5 B	
	1Q	0.0		0.0		62.8 B		28.6 B		41.1 B	
	MD	0.0		0.0		47.9 B		22.3		34.6	
	3Q	0.0		0.0		36.0 •		18.7 •		29.1 •	
	LO	0.0		0.0		11.2		9.2		16.0	
A) Relative To CIP Index..											
1. Your Risk Premium Return - US 90-Day TBills		-	-	53.85	-	28.84	-	18.73	-	20.58	-
2. Risk Premium Of CIP Index At Your Beta Level		-	-	54.90	-	35.45	-	23.89	-	22.61	-
3. Your Alpha, Or Superior Return. (Lines 1-2)		-	-	-0.5	-	-6.61	-	-5.16	-	-2.03	-
4. Standard Error Of Alpha		-	-	7.27	-	3.49	-	2.75	-	2.58	-
5. Your RAR, Or Alpha/Beta		-	-	-1.14	-	-6.83	-	-5.48	-	-2.15	-
B) Relative To The S&P 500											
1. Your Risk Premium		-	-	53.98	-	28.91	-	18.78	-	20.61	-
2. Risk Premium Of S&P 500 At Your Beta Level		-	-	3.54	-	11.13	-	6.79	-	7.90	-
3. Your Alpha, Or Superior Return. (Lines 1-2)		-	-	50.44	-	17.78	-	11.98	-	12.71	-
4. Standard Error Of Alpha		-	-	18.46	-	11.97	-	8.45	-	7.65	-
5. Your RAR, Or AlphaBeta (*)		-	-	355.65	-	35.58	-	18.34	-	29.13	-
6. RAR Of CIP Vs. S&P500.. (B)		-	-	269.40	-	57.51	-	30.07	-	43.20	-
7. Your % Rank/Num Portfolios.						78% / 72		76% / 66		75% / 51	

Amid debate as to their value, the adoption of risk-adjusted returns appears to have been less widespread than more basic risk measures. InterSec were one performance measurer to adopt the approach, as evidenced in their 1986 InterPerf product, illustrated in Table 8.1. Using the Jensen measure, InterSec described risk-adjusted return as the 'bottom line performance measure'. However, in a comparative report of performance measurement offerings commissioned by InterSec, Quantec commented that this did not seem to be 'useful information' to the ultimate owners of the funds.

Limitations of risk values

Key reasons for the lack of full acceptance of the volatility-based measures of risk include concerns about the basis of the calculations and their statistical significance. These aspects should also be borne in mind when attempting to interpret results. Key points are:

- The assumption that portfolio characteristics (beta, R-squared, etc) are constant over the measurement period. The longer the measurement period, the less likely this is to be true, and the less relevant the measure to the present portfolio.

- On the other hand, the regression approach needs sufficient observations to give reliable estimates of these values. The smaller the number of observations, the greater the standard error in the estimates. This is particularly true of alpha which is notoriously difficult to estimate reliably (even assuming that an 'abnormal return' is being achieved in reality).

There is therefore a trade-off between relevance and reliability. Figures quoted in US performance measurement services can be based on anything from 1 year of monthly returns to 5 years of quarterly returns. Frequently, betas based on multiple time-periods can be quoted in one report. In the UK, performance measurement has historically been no more frequent than quarterly, leading to limited availability of data for historical variability analysis. Monthly data is really required for the analysis to be meaningful, with a minimum of 2 years' data being used to estimate beta, etc.

One way round this is to analyse the current portfolio for risk factors as opposed to using historical returns. This clearly involves going down to stock level. Stock level betas for example are fairly widely available and can be used to construct a weighted average portfolio beta. This has the advantage that it is a much more accurate measure of the responsiveness of the current portfolio to market movements and allows risk to be measured correctly as a current/future phenomenon. However, this again can really only be done in a single equity market.

A further concern is the relevance of the market index against which the regression is taking place. For a single country, single asset class portfolio with a market index benchmark, R-squared can be quite close to 1 and therefore the beta values fairly reliable. Even for globally invested, single asset class portfolios (e.g. with an MSCI EAFE brief) the analysis can be meaningful, although currency factors and significant weighting differences from the index can reduce significance.

When it comes to globally invested, multi-asset class portfolios, such as UK Pension Funds, there is no recognised market index against which to analyse. Risk measures for parts of the fund may be interesting, but do not tell the Trustees much about their overall fund. This is part of the reason why industry bodies and practitioners in the UK have not recommended going beyond the level of 'total variability' in any analysis.

So if the single-factor measures of risk are not up to the job, what alternative approaches are available?

Multi-dimensional models

One aspect of the problem is that a simple linear model is being used to try to represent what is in fact quite a complex process. As computing power has permitted, this has led to the development of multi-variate models to attempt to explain sources of risk in more detail and to assist in portfolio investment decisions. There are two basic approaches to this.

The first, the 'Markowitz model', is essentially a multi-variate version of the CAPM. It involves estimating the covariances between all the asset classes under consideration and in fact in some cases this has been extended to individual stocks. These estimates have to be based on historical data as for the single-factor model and as there are many parameters involved, availability of data is even more critical. Once estimated, the models are often used to estimate the variability of returns from particular asset choices or indeed to find the optimal asset allocation through an 'efficient frontier' approach. That is, to maximise the expected return for a given level of risk (variability). This can be based either on historical or projected returns. Monte Carlo simulation can be used with these models to get a better understanding of the range of possible outcomes rather than just an 'optimal' portfolio.

Criticisms of the Markowitz approach are that long histories of data are required to estimate the covariance matrix and this in itself means that the estimates will be slow to adapt to actual changes in the underlying relationships between asset classes or individual assets. For more than just a few assets, the number of covariances to be estimated becomes very large and estimate errors may be high. Also for investors wanting to model at the security level, introducing new companies becomes a problem.

The second approach is multiple factor modelling and this has been adopted specifically by BARRA. In this approach, the number of possible variables is reduced by concentrating on fundamental common factors which are good at explaining movements in asset values. The responsiveness of each security to these common factors is then calculated. There are two parts to the model – returns and risk.

Returns $R = X \times f + u$

where

R = vector of asset excess returns

X = matrix of asset exposures

f = vector of factor returns

u = vector of stock specific returns (unexplained residual)

Risk $V = X \times F \times X^T + W$

where

V = covariance matrix of asset risks

F = factor covariance matrix

W = matrix of specific variances

Factors are selected which explain the risk or volatility of individual stocks: for example, size, share turnover, financial structure, growth orientation, industrial sectors. The amount of a company's risk explained by each factor is determined by its 'exposure' to that factor and this is updated regularly based on fundamental analysis and complex regression. The models can then be used to analyse a current or proposed portfolio's risk characteristics as well as attribute its return to the various factors.

The advantages of this over the Markowitz model are that it reduces dramatically the number of covariances that need to be estimated and also allows the model to be more responsive to changes in characteristics of stocks and markets. The factors may also be more intuitive to the portfolio manager or investment analyst and therefore more useful for portfolio selection.

However, there are still a large number of parameters to be estimated and estimate error is likely to be significant. This leads to concern as to the statistical validity of some of the conclusions that are drawn. Also, although multiple-market models do exist, the principal application of this approach is probably still for a single market or certainly a single asset class portfolio.

Finally, both of these multi-variate approaches are still wedded to return volatility as the definition of risk and are almost certainly too complex to be of value in quantifying and explaining risk for a total fund to trustees or plan sponsors.

Developments in the UK

Outside the USA, risk measures have been treated with a degree of scepticism, particularly risk-adjusted returns. This scepticism was reflected even more strongly in the UK where apart from manager use of the BARRA type models, none of the above risk measures, single or multi-dimensional, has yet been adopted in the leading performance measurement products. Despite the original IIMR recommendation that volatility or standard deviation of total returns is a useful statistic, even this measure is not widely used and performance has concentrated on the 'return dimension'.

This is partly due to fairly strong views in the UK that risk, particularly in relation to pension funds, is a multi-faceted concept which is not properly represented by historical measures based on variability. For example, Hager (1980) describes risk more in terms of a fund's long-term ability to match its salary-linked liabilities. He concludes:

It seems fairly clear that the use of such measures for risk as standard deviation and mean absolute deviation which are common in the US are totally inappropriate in the UK, because large fluctuations in asset values do not mean that the UK pension fund is running high levels of risk. Indeed, if one assumes that all of its liabilities are salary-related, a fund could show large fluctuations in asset values and yet still cover its liabilities providing that the returns on the investments were closely linked to the changes in salaries.

With this in mind, the US style analysis falls down in that, for a pension fund, the 'risk-free asset' is not an asset with guaranteed return and low or zero variability. Investing in such an asset would in fact lead to a high risk of the fund being unable to match its liabilities due to lack of return. It is argued that a healthy exposure to equities is essential to reduce this risk, despite the additional volatility that this implies.

Hager's concern is essentially that returns fall short of requirements to meet liabilities. In other words, volatility is only a problem when combined with high probability of negative cash flow. A fund does not want to be forced to sell assets at the bottom of the market in order to make up for a shortfall in income. Volatility alone is not always a true indicator of this risk. Consider, for example, the relative merits of long and short gilts when the requirement is to provide for a long-term monetary liability. Since gilt prices are determined largely by interest rate expectations, the prices of long gilts will be much more volatile in the short term than those of short gilts. However if a 20-year gilt is chosen to

Table 8.2 Real returns & standard deviation (SD) in the UK 1919–1990+

	Gilts		UK Equities		Treasury Bills *	
	Average Real Return	SD	Average Real Return	SD	Average Real Return	SD
1 year	2.1	15.3	9.9	24.6	0.5	5.6
3 year cum	1.7	9.0	8.1	13.2	0.4	4.7
5 year cum	1.3	7.0	7.6	9.8	0.2	4.3
10 year cum	0.7	5.2	6.5	6.0	-0.4	3.2
15 year cum	0.1	4.3	5.9	4.7	-0.8	2.1
20 year cum	-0.5	3.0	5.5	2.7	-0.8	1.6

+ Source BZW Research Ltd (except T-Bills prior to 1945)
* 1924 - 90

match a 20-year liability and held to maturity, then this volatility is irrelevant and the return is guaranteed. By contrast, short gilts may display less price volatility, but the investor is now subject to re-investment risk, that is, uncertainty over the prevailing interest rates at the time of re-investment. So the timing of liabilities or cash flow requirements must be taken into account.

When inflation is brought into the equation as a variable, 'riskiness' can be viewed very differently. A comparison of real returns and variability for different classes of investment illustrates this point and also reaffirms the importance of time horizons.

Table 8.2 shows the rolling period real returns (1, 3, 5, 10, 15 and 20 years) for UK Equities, Gilts and Treasury Bills. This is over the period 1919 to 1990 (from 1924 for Treasury Bills). The average of the 1 year returns is the most often cited figure and the table shows that over the whole period UK equities have produced a real return of close to 10% with a standard deviation of almost 25%. The equivalent figures for gilts are a real return of 2% per annum and a standard deviation of 15% whilst those for T-Bills are 0.5% and 6%.

These figures conform to accepted theory that equities provide a higher return but at greater 'risk', i.e. higher variability of returns. Looking at the longer term rolling periods the ordering remains the same but both returns and standard deviations reduce. Over 20 year periods, UK equities produced an average real return of 5.5% per annum with gilts and Treasury Bills disappointing at only –0.5% and –0.8% per annum respectively. Moreover, the standard deviation for UK Equity returns over this time-frame actually falls below that of gilts!

It is results such as these which provide the strong case for equities as the best asset for pension fund investment in the UK where the liability profile is often 20 years or more. If risk is redefined as the probability of producing a

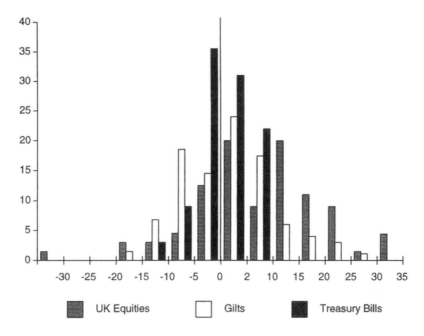

40
35
30
25
20
15
10
5
0

-30 -25 -20 -15 -10 -5   0   2   10   15   20   25   30   35

■ UK Equities   ☐ Gilts   ■ Treasury Bills

8.3 Distribution frequency (%) – rolling 3–year real returns in the UK 1924/90.

negative real return then UK equities must be rated the least risky of the three asset classes on the evidence of the last 70 years.

Essentially the introduction of inflation steers the probabilities of achieving real returns over a prolonged period in favour of equities. Taking Fig. 8.3 for example, the standard deviation of equity returns is much wider but the probability of achieving say a 5% real return is much greater than for either gilts or T-bills.

This concept that risk is based on the probability of failing to meet objectives has been explored more mathematically in papers presented to the Faculty of Actuaries in Scotland. Firstly in Clarkson and Plymen (1987) and subsequently in Clarkson (1989) it is argued that 'investment risk as measured by the variability of return is essentially irrelevant in the practical management of investment portfolios and that attention should be focused instead on using advanced analytical techniques to improve the expected return'.

The latter paper develops a general theory of investment risk based on the practical conclusions of the former, which concentrated on equity portfolios. It also compares the approach with the MPT approaches of Markowitz, Sharpe, Rosenberg and others. The authors' criticisms of these MPT approaches are numerous, but essentially boil down to their preoccupation with variability as a proxy for risk. They use examples similar to those above to show that variability is irrelevant for all but the shortest of periods and that 'return dominates' over the longer term, particularly in inflationary times.

Clarkson's general theory is based on the following axioms (simplified from the paper):

1. Investment risk is a function both of the probability of the return being below a certain threshold and also of the severity of the financial consequences arising from these values of return.

2. If the probability density function of return, p(r), is known, then investment risk, R, can be expressed as:

$$R = \int_{-\infty}^{L} W(L-r)p(r)dr$$

    where

    L = the value of return above which no adverse consequences arise

    W = a weighting function which defines the scale of the financial consequences of a return less than L – the lower the return, the greater the weight

3. For investments with the same expected return, an investor will prefer the investment with the lowest risk.

4. Each investor has a threshold of risk, R_0, and will not make an investment which involves a value of risk higher than R_0.

5. An investor will choose between all possible investments by maximising the return subject to the risk not exceeding R_0.

6. Different investors may differ in their degree of aversion to risk by using different functions W() and/or different thresholds of risk R_0.

The main characteristics of this approach are that it concentrates on downside risk only and that it includes a weighting function for different levels of under-performance to allow the investor to quantify his attitudes to risk. This concept clearly has applicability to pension fund trustees attempting to ensure that liabilities are matched and finance directors keen to ensure that company pension fund contributions do not have to increase unexpectedly. It will be interesting to see how this theoretical approach develops and whether it will have sufficient practical application to become a standard tool in performance measurement.

Other aspects of risk

It is not surprising that this area has been explored by actuaries. The concept of matching liabilities and the risks of mis-match are basic to the insurance industry. This is not to say that volatility, including short-term volatility, is not relevant in assessment of risk in this context. Legal and accounting conventions can be very important and increase the importance of short-term volatility.

In the USA, the FASB rules require companies to 'mark-to-market' their projected pension costs for inclusion in their annual accounts and top-up any shortfall on an annual basis. A short-term downturn in fund values can therefore have a direct and immediate impact on company profitability even though the real liabilities are long term. Pressure through European Directives to introduce minimum solvency standards could have a similar impact in the UK, forcing funds to adopt more bond-orientated asset allocation strategies which protect against short-term volatility. However, at the time of writing, there was significant resistance to the imposition of such constraints in the UK, both from the companies affected and from the actuarial profession, who point principally to the increase in long-term risk which could result from such short-term constraints as described above.

Within continental Europe, the argument works the other way round as there has historically been a much more conservative attitude to investing pension assets. An example of this can be taken from the Netherlands pension industry, where traditionally funds invested a high proportion of their assets in private loans, with relatively modest but stable returns. This investment policy arose partly from the fact that, due to low inflation, funds set their targets in nominal terms, say 4% annual growth. There was little risk of failing to meet this return, but in fact a sizeable opportunity cost through not investing in 'riskier assets' such as equities.

Accounting practice determined that fixed interest investments were carried at book cost, however, while equities were 'marked-to-market'. Thus, provided a coupon in excess of 4% was available, fixed interest investments held no downside risk. Equities, by contrast, could suffer considerable negative returns over any single accounting period and lead to a short term loss which had to be made good.

In Japan a similar minimum return requirement is set with any shortfall in an accounting period needing to be made up by contributions. Thus short term volatility becomes critical for the underlying plan sponsor.

The different perspectives on risk and the various investment, legal and accounting requirements, can thus produce conflicting optimum asset allocations. Final optimum fund distribution may therefore be a compromise solution.

Proper analysis of risk requires an understanding of the time horizons involved, the liability profile and hence the liquidity requirements. This turns risk correctly into an analysis of the future and assumptions need to be made about the expected returns in each asset class and the uncertainty relating to these expected returns as well as their cross-correlations. Asset/liability models and asset allocation models attempt to find the optimum allocation of assets to achieve the desired minimum return with the maximum certainty. They are inherently complex and suffer from the usual 'garbage in, garbage out' syndrome. They also tend to use historical measures of variability and correlation as their input. However, at least they are addressing the concept of risk in a way which reflects its real meaning to Pension Fund Trustees. Performance measurement and attribution can then be used to monitor the success of the asset allocation decisions and validate the model assumptions over time. Once broad asset allocation decisions have been made, there can be further risks associated with the implementation of the strategy.

Manager selection or performance risk is associated with the uncertainty of achieving the required return in particular asset classes. This can be controlled at a cost, for example by indexing and accepting the opportunity cost or alternatively by paying a premium for portfolio insurance. Some results from real experience are given in Chapters 9 and 10 and illustrate the dimension of this extra risk.

Benchmark risk has two aspects. Firstly, for the fund, the basic benchmark or asset allocation chosen may not in fact be optimal. The downside for this risk can be limited by generous funding and this may or may not represent an opportunity cost to the company or plan sponsor. Secondly, additional risk can be introduced for the manager. In implementing policies to match or beat a benchmark the manager is taking a commercial risk, as well as incurring a performance risk on behalf of the client. Success in beating the benchmark will allow the manager to promote their skills and, potentially, gain new business. Failure to beat the benchmark is likely to produce the opposite effect and can undermine the commercial success of the, fund management, business.

The issues

The desire to measure risk, despite the difficulties inherent in the process of defining it in the first place, led to the acceptance of a simplifying assumption – that investment returns displayed normal distribution characteristics and therefore standard deviation could be used as a satisfactory proxy for risk. For many practical purposes this has been an acceptable working assumption and has allowed the development of a whole body of investment theory but the underlying simplifying assumption is ignored at our peril.

Even where such a proxy for risk is acceptable there are still reservations about combining risk and return to produce a single figure 'risk–adjusted' return. Many practitioners believe that the two aspects should be kept separate and analysed as two distinct elements of the investment process.

For many situations the simplifying assumption is not acceptable and different definitions of risk are required. Such alternative concepts of risk present difficulties, however when it comes to numerical measurement. Although attempts by Clarkson et al have been made to overcome this problem, they have not been incorporated into the performance measurement process.

Where the assessment of future risk is tackled it is in the form of Monte Carlo simulations which may be incorporated into the asset/liability modelling processes used by consulting actuaries. Even these processes rely on relatively simplified data of returns, volatilities and correlations which limit their reliability as modelling tools.

In the final analysis the search for a simple numerical solution to the problem of risk may be a futile one. The recognition of risk in its various forms is the key factor and even a qualitative assessment may be of more value than an over-simplified numerical one and is certainly better than totally ignoring the problem.

The results

The previous two sections have examined the history and development of performance measurement and the practical problems encountered in the process. This section examines the results achieved by funds over the past twenty years and the consequent developments. For the most part we make use of data accumulated by The WM Company since 1974, supplemented by other sources where data is available. By examining the actual performance of a universe of real funds we can see examples of how results can be analysed and how this information can lead to changes in the structure of funds and the methods of management.

In Chapter 9 the results of a universe of UK pension funds are analysed. We compare portfolio returns with index benchmarks and the evolution of fund returns to create peer group or universe benchmarks in line with BAI and IIMR recommendations. Returns from the major asset classes are compared and the shift in asset allocation which has resulted from both passive and active cash flows allocation patterns.

Experience over the period has led to changes in the investment management process and these developments are examined in Chapter 10. This includes an examination of the move from single and multi-balanced managers to the complex multi-specialist manager structures adopted by some funds. We also examine the emergence of index tracking and universe tracking as trustees and plan sponsors become more concerned with poor performance.

Although concentrating our analysis on UK experience we examine the differences in development seen in other regions. These are sometimes the result of different achieved asset class returns but may also arise from differing legal and accounting practices. Different industry structures and cultural environments have also contributed to a different evolution. These issues are addressed in Chapter 11.

Finally, Chapter 12 explores some of the myths and misunderstandings which have prevailed over the years. We examine the evidence from the results to substantiate or explode the myths and to clarify the misunderstandings.

Evidence of universe results

Introduction

Since the 1960s the performance of pension funds has been closely monitored in the USA and the UK. By the early 1970s a sufficiently large number of funds were being measured by the leading practitioners on both sides of the Atlantic to establish universes of funds which might be regarded as representative of pension fund experience within those assets and markets in which the funds were invested.

Much of the data on fund performance is proprietary with specific performance measurement companies monitoring their own client base. It is also difficult to establish a continuous history of data on a consistent basis. Furthermore the benchmarks have not always been in existence for a long time or have been changed to meet changing circumstances. Very often the evolution of the benchmark follows the investment patterns of funds rather than precedes them. For example the creation of emerging market indices was in response to evidence that many funds were investing in these markets and a satisfactory benchmark was required to monitor performance.

With these limitations in mind this chapter examines the performance of pension funds in the UK, for the most part. On such evidence as is available, the UK experience within asset classes is not so different from the experience in other countries with important investment funds. The results over the past twenty years are examined and the shifts in investment patterns are discussed with the main focus being the UK. Chapter 11 looks at the different characteristics of pension funds in other areas. The availability of such a long history of returns from a comprehensive universe enables the investor to establish realistic expectations and to set meaningful benchmarks and performance targets.

UK experience since 1975

Table 9.1 shows the results of the WM UK pension fund universe for the twenty year period 1975–94. For comparison the returns for a suitable index benchmark are also shown alongside the major asset categories, where available.

Over the whole period the four major asset classes in which the universe was invested were UK & Overseas Equities, UK Bonds and UK Property. In 1982 Index-Linked Bonds were introduced by the Bank of England and were quickly taken up by pension funds. From 1986 further overseas diversification occurred in both Bonds and Property. The returns shown for cash/other investments include not only short-term cash deposits but also various unquoted investments and miscellaneous assets including commodities and works of art.

Over the twenty years the returns achieved by UK pension funds have been exceptional at 17.2% pa. This compares with the annualised rate of inflation (as represented in the UK by the Retail Price Index – RPI) of 8.6% pa. Thus pension funds have achieved a real return of over 8% pa.

By applying a standardised technique of performance measurement in a consistent way over an extended period we are able to obtain reasonably accurate information on the actual returns achieved by UK pension funds, a major financial resource within the economy. Without the application of such performance measurement the only basic, accounting, information we might have is that the value of pension funds had risen from £x bn in 1976 to £y bn in 1994 – factually correct but with little value in assessing the efficiency of the pension fund industry in managing such an important resource.

But how does this return compare with a benchmark? For pension funds as a whole there is no acceptable benchmark; indeed the returns achieved by a universe of funds such as the WM pension fund universe or the CAPS universe are themselves used as a benchmark. In the USA an attempt was made to establish a multi-markets index representing the capitalisations of all the major asset classes in which pension funds invested. The proportions of asset classes within such a multi-markets index bore little relationship to the proportions of those assets actually held by the funds, however, and it is not widely accepted as a performance benchmark. Even the MMI produced by First Chicago, which weighted the assets such as to produce a mean variance with similar risk to the 'typical' pension fund, has not been widely adopted as a benchmark.

When assessing the overall returns therefore it is more usual to use a target return as a benchmark; for example a 3% pa real return. Over this period UK pension funds have exceeded even the most demanding of such targets.

We can, however, use index benchmarks for each asset class and compare the pension fund returns against index returns. For example in the table the returns on UK equities can be compared with the returns shown for the FT–SE Actuaries All Share Index. The data shows that the returns achieved are closely

Table 9.1 WM UK pension fund universe returns 1975/94

	UK Equities	Index	Overseas Equities	Index	North America	Continental Europe	Japan	Total (ex Japan)	Other Intl. Equities	Total Bonds	UK Bonds
1975	151.0	151.2	47.0	51.6	39.0	39.0	39.0	39.0	39.0	39.0	39.0
1976	-0.8	2.2	24.1	38.9						15.0	15.0
1977	49.0	48.9	-20.5	-12.7						45.0	45.0
1978	6.9	8.4	12.9	11.7						-1.5	-1.5
1979	8.0	10.4	-12.1	2.8						4.9	4.9
1980	33.3	35.2	28.9	17.4						20.7	20.7
1981	14.3	13.7	16.3	21.9						2.4	2.4
1982	30.7	29.1	27.3	37.9						52.6	52.6
1983	28.4	29.0	40.5	32.4						16.2	16.2
1984	29.8	31.9	21.1	32.6						10.4	10.4
1985	19.8	20.3	10.8	12.8						12.6	12.6
1986	25.9	27.4	37.2	40.8						12.9	12.5
1987	7.1	7.9	-18.5	-9.3						15.3	16.4
1988	10.4	11.5	23.4	31.3						8.1	8.2
1989	36.0	36.0	40.3	31.0						8.8	7.4
1990	-9.8	-9.7	-27.3	-32.1	-20.3	-22.5	-42.7		-27.4	5.3	7.9
1991	20.0	20.7	20.9	23.4	32.8	13.9	12.0	32.7	25.5	19.6	18.2
1992	20.8	20.4	19.7	17.6	32.4	18.3	-0.9	37.5	21.0	23.1	19.1
1993	27.9	28.3	39.4	25.9	13.5	35.4	30.0	95.3	53.1	21.6	25.1
1994	-5.6	-5.8	-3.7	0.9	-5.1	-1.4	14.7	-17.0	-11.1	-7.0	-8.4
1975/94	22.1	22.9	14.1	16.9						15.4	15.3

Table 9.1 continued

Index	Overseas Bonds	Index	UK Index-Linked	Index	Cash/Other Investment	Total (ex Property)	Total Property	UK Property	Index	Overseas Property	Total Assets
36.8					11.0	81.9	18.0	18.0			64.5
13.7					9.7	5.3	4.8	4.8			5.2
36.3					10.2	38.5	21.1	21.1			35.0
-1.2					8.9	5.0	16.5	16.5			7.1
5.1					11.8	5.6	19.4	19.4			8.3
19.6					15.0	28.5	14.5	14.5	9.7		25.9
4.5					12.7	11.2	14.4	14.4	13.0		11.8
41.6			16.6		13.3	33.9	8.9	8.9	1.0		28.6
13.6			0	0.5	9.3	25.6	8.7	8.7	12.7		22.9
8.9			5.8	5.5	1.5	21.5	12.3	12.3	5.6		20.3
11.9			0.2	1.5	19.9	16.1	3.6	3.6	7.4		14.5
11.5	26.0	18.4	5.1	6.8	11.6	24.5	7.1	7.3	4.3	5.8	22.5
15.2	-1.0	-11.5	6.2	6.6	8.1	2.4	14.7	19.4	14.9	-14.1	3.4
6.7	4.6	9.5	13.0	12.0	9.2	12.1	30.6	32.8	30.4	10.7	13.8
8.2	17.4	20.4	14.3	14.5	14.2	31.6	18.9	18.2	19.3	24.2	30.3
9.6	-1.4	-7.6	3.9	5.8	12.6	-10.8	-8.0	-7.5	-5.4	-12.7	-10.6
16.1	21.0	19.6	4.9	5.4	10.4	18.8	-1.7	-1.8	-1.8	-0.2	16.9
18.6	29.1	30.0	17.8	16.5	13.2	20.3	-1.1	-1.3	0.3	0.8	18.6
20.9	17.9	14.2	20.7	18.9	9.5	29.0	16.4	18.8	12.3	-6.1	28.2
-6.2	-5.3	-7.0	-8.1		5.4	-4.8	12.3	13.3	19.1	-7.6	-3.9
13.9					10.8	18.4	11.2	11.7			17.1

in line with the index. In most years the returns fall marginally short of the index, commonly attributed to the costs incurred in running a live fund which are not incurred by an index. Such an outcome is not surprising given the significant proportion of total UK equities outstanding which would be represented by the pension fund universe. Over the whole period the annualised returns emerge at just 0.8% pa lower than the index which is probably a reasonable indication of trading costs.

When we compare the returns on overseas equities a different picture emerges. Annual differences can be quite marked and the annualised returns for the 20 years shows a shortfall of nearer 2½% pa. Whilst this can be partially attributable to trading costs the annual variations indicate that the pension funds have not held fully representative portfolios in overseas equities.

From our detailed knowledge of these portfolios we do, in fact, know that they are often weighted across countries in a very different way to the weights within the index. This tends to be a major source of difference in the returns achieved. Furthermore the representation within countries tends to be limited to only a few companies when compared with the index.

Thus the overall returns from overseas equities in the table vary significantly from the index and are seen to be almost 15 points lower or higher than the index. Such variation could justifiably raise the question of the suitability of the index as a benchmark! A benchmark which recognises the actual investment patterns of funds might be more useful.

UK pension fund universe

We therefore turn our attention to the evolution of such a benchmark in the UK and the experience of funds relative to it. In the UK the two major universes which evolved were the CAPS universe and the WM pension fund universe. Major overlap exists between the two with the former having wide coverage among smaller funds and the latter being dominated by the mega-funds of the formerly nationalised industries.

Figure 9.1 shows the WM universe returns for each year 1975–94 with the ranges of returns of the constituent funds. The range is truncated at the 5th and 95th percentile in order to exclude exceptional outriders. The inter-quartile (25th–75th percentile) range is also shown and the median and weighted average points are indicated.

The range of returns shown is quite wide in any one year from a minimum of 8% in 1988 to the, exceptional, 53% in 1975. Excluding that year the range can still be almost 20% as seen in 1977. In most years, however, the range falls within the 8% to 12% band. The inter-quartile range is, generally, less varied and 3% to 5% covers most years.

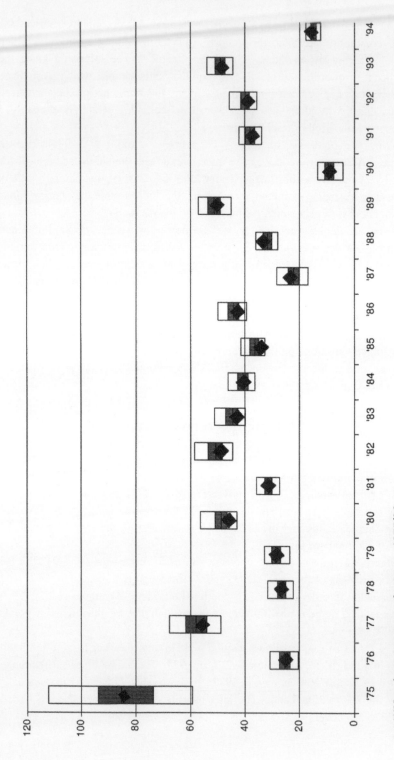

9.1 WM universe range of returns 1975/94.

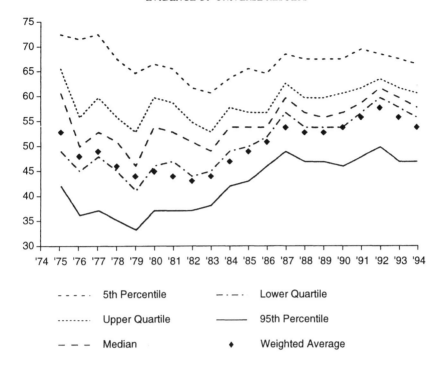

- - - - -	5th Percentile	— · — ·	Lower Quartile
....	Upper Quartile	————	95th Percentile
— — —	Median	♦	Weighted Average

9.2 Asset distribution – UK equities.

Figures published by CAPS for the period 1984–93 have shown a similar pattern with the inter-quartile range being between 3% and 5% in each year.

The difference between the median and the weighted average is a reflection of the impact of the larger funds in the sample when their returns have differed from smaller funds. To understand why this might occur it is necessary to examine the range of asset distributions and the range of returns within asset classes. This should also explain the overall range of returns.

Figures 9.2 to 9.6 show the ranges of asset distribution of the major asset classes within the WM universe. Clearly the funds within the universe held very diverse mixtures of assets. Among the major asset classes, for example UK equities, the difference could be over 30% between the 5th and 95th percentile fund when ranked by exposure to that asset class. This is clearly a potential source of difference in total fund returns. In order for this potential to be realised, however, the returns on the major asset classes also need to be very different. Fund A may have 70% UK Equities 25% UK Bonds while Fund B has 60% UK Equities 40% UK Bonds. In a year such as 1975 (see Table 9.1) such a difference would have a marked impact on total return whereas in 1977 the impact would be small. Asset allocation was clearly an important factor in the wide range of returns displayed for 1975.

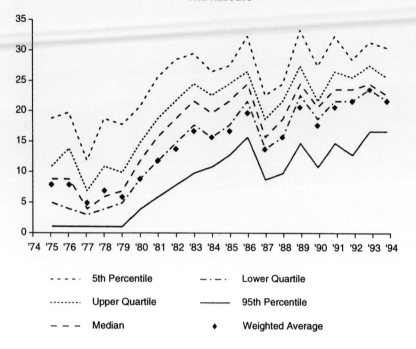

9.3 Asset distribution – overseas equities.

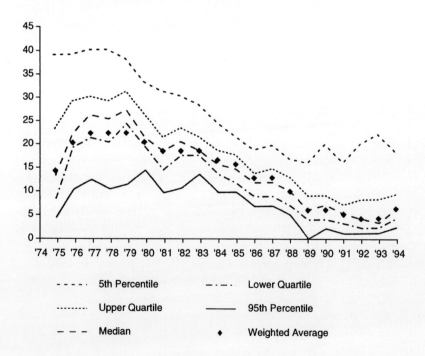

9.4 Asset distribution – UK bonds.

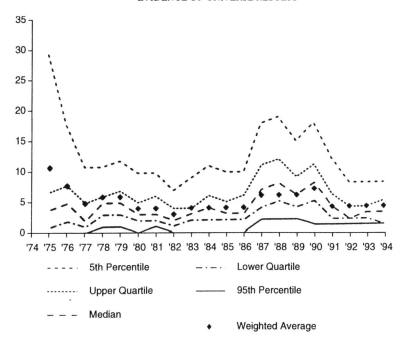

9.5 Asset distribution – cash/other investments.

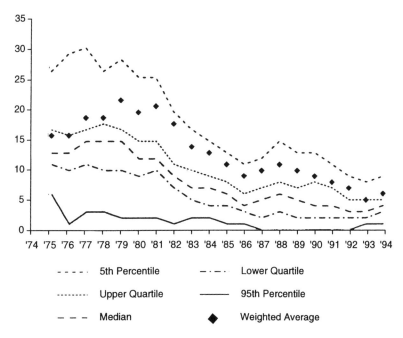

9.6 Asset distribution – total property.

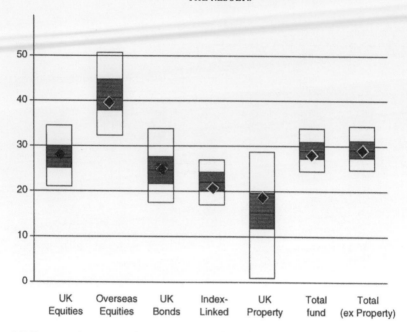

9.7 Range of returns within asset class 1993.

The asset distribution charts also give the clue to the difference in weighted average return and median. The charts for UK and overseas equities show the weighted average plotting below the median line, indicating that larger funds held lower proportions in equities than the median fund. On the other hand the property chart shows the weighted average plotting higher, larger funds held more property. When equity and property returns differed the weighted average differed from the median at total fund level.

For most years, however, the main source of variation in total fund returns is the variation in returns within the major asset classes. Figure 9.7 shows the typical range of returns in any one year on the major asset classes held by pension funds. (The data is for 1993 but the range is similar in any year.)

In any one year the returns on UK equities, for example, could differ by as much as 12% between 5th and 95th percentile funds. Even wider ranges could be experienced in the other major asset classes as shown in the chart. The most consistent source of difference in total returns across funds within the universe has, therefore, been the difference in returns on the asset classes within the fund. In some years this has been further exacerbated by the different asset mix held.

Changing asset mix

As Fig. 9.2 to 9.6 showed the asset mix has not been static over the period and the weighted average exposure has shifted markedly over the twenty years.

Table 9.2 End year asset mix – % total assets

	UK Equities	Overseas Equities	Total Bonds	UK Linked	Cash/Other Investment	Total (ex Prop.)	Total Property	Total Assets
1975	53	8	15		8	84	16	100
1976	48	8	21		7	84	16	100
1977	49	5	23		4	81	19	100
1978	46	7	23		5	81	19	100
1979	44	6	23		5	78	22	100
1980	45	9	21		5	80	20	100
1981	44	12	19		4	79	21	100
1982	43	14	19	3	3	82	18	100
1983	44	17	19	3	3	86	14	100
1984	47	16	17	3	4	87	13	100
1985	49	17	16	3	4	89	11	100
1986	51	20	13	3	4	91	9	100
1987	54	14	13	3	6	90	10	100
1988	53	16	10	3	7	89	11	100
1989	53	21	8	2	6	90	10	100
1990	54	18	9	3	7	91	9	100
1991	56	21	9	2	4	92	8	100
1992	58	22	8	3	3	94	6	100
1993	56	24	8	3	4	95	5	100
1994	54	23	9	4	4	94	6	100

Table 9.2 shows the asset mix of the WM pension fund universe at each year end since end 1975.

In the early years 1974–79 equity exposure was reduced from the 60% level to 50%, perhaps as a reaction to the traumatic collapse and recovery experienced in 1974–75. Bonds and property were both increased over this period. In both cases it resulted from positive cash flow allocation decisions and not from relative performance.

Since 1979, and the abolition of exchange controls in the UK, equity exposure increased steadily to 80% at end 1993. Bonds fell from 23% to 8%, of which only half now consists of UK bonds compared to 1979 when bond exposure was all in the UK. Property has fallen from 22% to 5%.

Relative performance and cash flow decisions both contributed to these declines. The modest reversal of this decline seen in 1994 was the result of strong positive cash flow in the case of bonds and strong relative performance in the case of property.

UK pension funds have clearly made a major commitment to equity investment over the past twenty years and have reduced conventional bond exposure to under 10%. This is in contrast to pension funds in other countries, an issue which will be explored in Chapter 11.

Apart from the high overall returns achieved over this twenty year period the main features of the UK pension fund sector are the diversity of asset distributions and of returns achieved within assets. The latter has been a cause of concern in some funds and the uncertainty surrounding the likely returns on a fund's assets have led to an interest in indexation within asset classes and consensus asset allocation across assets. Some of these issues are discussed in the next chapter.

Again the consistent application of performance measurement and analysis enables us to make judgements about the efficiency with which UK pension assets have been managed. We are also able to analyse the source of any deviation from a defined benchmark experienced by the individual funds within the universe.

Over the past twenty years the pension fund industry has monitored their performance and reacted to the evidence as it has emerged. As more refined analysis becomes available, and more evidence accumulates, effective management responses should result.

The issues

Within the UK pension fund industry there has been growing concern at the high exposure to equity assets. The superior returns from equities over the long term (usually agreed to be twenty years or more) are not in dispute. The main concern is that pension funds are maturing rapidly with the result that cash outflows will start to exceed cash income (from both investment income and contributions) in the near future. In such circumstances the volatility of equities, equated with high risk by many, makes equities unsuitable.

Whilst it is certainly the case that some funds are now in the situation described, the apparent lack of positive cash flow of the UK pension fund sector in total is deceptive. Many funds have been in such healthy surpluses that contributions, particularly on the part of the employer, or plan sponsor, have been reduced or stopped completely. The large majority of funds therefore remain well short of maturity and could afford to maintain a high equity structure.

The exceptional returns achieved on equities may not, of course, continue and may even, as in 1994, produce negative overall returns. It is notable however that the negative returns on UK equities in 1994 were still better than the returns from UK bonds and index-linked stocks, both regarded as the 'safer' option.

A further issue in the UK is the contention that competitive pressures in the fund management industry have forced funds into 'following the herd'. Although Fig. 9.2 to 9.6 in this chapter indicate some tendency to stay close to the industry median exposure for UK equities, the overall dispersion remains wide. There is little evidence that the range of asset allocations adopted by funds has narrowed over the past ten years. It is true, however, that UK pension funds as a whole have adopted a relatively high equity strategy when compared with other countries. Whether this is a reflection of a 'herd instinct' or simply a common wisdom is debatable. Most funds in the UK, until the recent emergence of money purchase schemes, have been final salary defined benefit schemes which imposes a very different liability on the fund than if the benefit was defined in nominal income terms. Moreover they have been immature in so far as the retired members have been heavily outnumbered by members in employment. Time will, inevitably, change this position and a different balance will be reached which may then require more diverse asset allocation across funds.

The investment management process

Introduction

The approach adopted by the owners of investment funds to the process of investment management has changed over the past thirty years. The major institutional holders of investment assets were the insurance and banking companies and these organisations had established teams of investment analysts and managers. They were responsible for the insurance funds or the banks' assets and were the obvious choice when wealthy individuals or pension fund plan sponsors were seeking professional management for their funds. In some cases, very large pools of assets might be managed by an 'in-house' team set up for the purpose.

In most cases the assets would be allocated to a single organisation but, in the USA in particular, the size of some funds soon pushed plan sponsors towards splitting the fund between two or more managers. The choice of manager was a major commitment for the fund and the evolution of performance measurement in the 1960s and 1970s quickly highlighted the variation in fund return which might occur as a result of manager selection.

Disillusionment with manager performance led to several developments in the fund management sector. In order to spread the risks of manager selection more funds chose to split their assets between two or more managers.

In the USA the discontent with the management performance of the major institutions spawned a new breed of specialist investment management boutiques, often created and staffed by personnel from the big institutions. In the UK this was less common and the sector rapidly became dominated by the merchant bank and stockbroking organisations with their experience of running investment and unit trusts.

A further response to unsatisfactory management performance was to constrain management risk by indexing large parts of the fund. Index funds were pioneered in the USA by Wells Fargo and after a slow start took off in the 1970s and 1980s.

This chapter examines these developments and some of the performance results which led to them and resulted from them.

Management selection risk

In Chapter 9 the range of returns was shown for the WM pension fund universe, demonstrating that in any one year the difference between the 5th percentile and the 95th percentile fund could be around 10%. Although variations in asset mix accounted for part of this range the range on returns within the major asset classes held was the most consistent source of difference. Effectively manager performance was an important source of the uncertainty of returns.

Over a longer period some of the random characteristics of manager performance in any single year would be ironed out and a lower range of returns might be expected. Table 10.1 shows that this indeed does happen. The 5th to 95th percentile range falls to 4.8% over 5 years and to 3.9% and 3.8% over 10 and 15 years respectively. The inter-quartile range also narrows and over half the funds will, typically, fall within a range of ± 1% of the median. Nevertheless these variations represent a considerable element of uncertainty when looking at the expected returns for a fund. A difference of 4% pa between a top performing fund and a bottom performing fund is of major importance to the funding capabilities of a pension fund for example.

These ranges are confirmed when we examine the performance of investment management organisations. Figure 10.1 shows the range of returns achieved by pension fund management organisations in the UK over the five year period 1989/93. The range of fund returns within each organisation and the

Table 10.1 Longer term range of returns – WM PF universe

Periods to 1993	Percentile					Wtd Avge
	95th	75th	50th	25th	5th	
5 Years	14.1	15.9	16.7	17.5	18.9	15.7
10 Years	13.9	15.2	16.0	16.7	17.8	15.2
15 Years	15.4	16.5	17.4	19.4	19.2	16.5

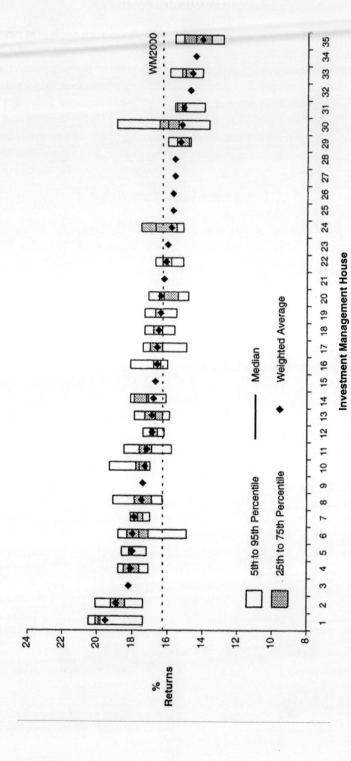

10.1 Weighted average comparison (total assets) – five years to 31 December 1993.

weighted average 'house' return is shown. The 5th to 95th percentile range is from 18.9% pa to 14.6% pa, very similar to the range shown for the total universe. These results highlight the extra uncertainty or risk confronting fund sponsors when selecting the manager for their funds. One response to this problem has been to diversify the risk by splitting the fund across more than one manager. The hope may be that all such selected managers will perform above average but the realistic expectation must be that a manager producing below average returns will be counter-balanced by one producing above average returns. In the UK this tendency to split funds has been confined, for the most part, to the larger funds. Small funds would find the higher management charges prohibitive. The managers tended to be given the same, balanced, brief. That is the allocation of the fund across assets and within asset classes was left to the discretion of the manager – sometimes within broad constraints dependent on the objectives of the fund.

In the USA this practice was also adopted but was quickly varied to incorporate the appointment of specialists to manage specific assets within the fund. An early manifestation was the appointment of separate equity and bond managers. Continued disappointment with the performance of general equity funds led to the splitting of the equity assets into specialist sub-sectors. Thus technology companies were identified as an area which could benefit from specialist knowledge and expertise and management boutiques specialising in this sector emerged to offer their services. Managers specialising in smaller companies, in cyclical companies, in growth companies or in value companies also materialised on the premise that by specialising they could engender superior performance.

Although such a concept had much to commend it in principle, in practice it has led to several problems. A major problem is that responsibility for the allocation of assets into the suitable investment areas reverts to the plan sponsor, in the absence of a specialist asset allocator. The proportions so allocated could be neutral in their impact by modelling the main benchmark index into suitably defined sub-sectors and allocating on a weighted basis. In practice many of these specialist sectors over-lap and it is difficult to define a neutral allocation.

A second problem is that the specialist managers have still to out-perform their specialist benchmark. Although there is some evidence that, in aggregate, the performance of specialist portfolios is better, relative to their own benchmark, than generalist portfolios, the range of returns can be even wider than for generalist portfolios. Manager selection risk remains a key factor and can only be overcome by a proliferation of managers. Thus some large USA pension funds can have up to 100 different managers.

There is little evidence that such a policy produces better overall returns for the fund than a simpler structure. It does, however, illustrate how performance measurement and analysis can stimulate change in the management process.

Table 10.2 Balanced funds v specialist funds 1988/92

	Weighted Average % Return					
	1988	1989	1990	1991	1992	5 Yr Ann'd
WM PF Universe	13.8	30.3	-10.6	16.9	18.6	13.0
Balanced funds	13.7	30.9	-10.2	17.5	20.1	13.5
(Number of funds)	(87)	(89)	(81)	(85)	(80)	
Specialist Funds	13.7	28.1	-10.4	16.8	17.9	12.4
(Number of Funds)	(15)	(16)	(19)	(20)	(33)	

In the UK the move down the specialist route has been less widespread and much less extreme in terms of sector definitions. As a result few funds in the UK can boast a list of managers in double digits. Those who have followed the specialist route have tended to restrict their equity portfolio sub-division into only a few categories. Small and larger companies, venture capital, and overseas companies is the most common split. The overseas sector can be further split by regional specialisation so Far East, N America and Europe portfolios may be established and, more recently, an emerging markets portfolio.

Again little hard evidence is available as to the efficacy of such specialist structures. The WM Company have published some studies comparing multi-managed funds with discretionary briefs with multi-managed funds with specialist briefs. On the basis of a limited sample and time period, as shown in Table 10.2, the discretionary route has been the more successful.

Given the limited number of funds in the sample it would be dangerous to draw firm conclusions. The analysis by The WM Company did, however, point up some clues to potential problems for specialist structures. A significant proportion of the difference in return was accounted for by what they term policy. That is the contribution from the different mix of assets held and the shifts in asset mix over the period. It would appear that the managers with discretion were able to adapt to market trends more successfully than the sponsors of the specialist funds. This, however, may not be a problem if the asset structure of the specialist funds has been determined to meet their specific requirements and flexible asset allocation was not an objective. More disconcerting was the fact that another cause of the shortfall in performance was the failure to achieve superior asset class returns. In other words the selection skills of the specialist managers in total did not prove to be superior to the skills of managers with a discretionary brief. Again this may be due to the allocation within equities of the specialist portfolios. For example an over-weight (relative to the benchmark) allocation to small companies or venture capital at a time when these areas under-performed could produce the result experienced. The specialist manager within that area may still be producing a result above his, specialist, benchmark.

International diversification

An important trend in most of the economies with a large investment industry has been the trend to international diversification. This was probably evident earliest in the UK. Even before the liberalisation of exchange controls in 1979 UK investment funds had significant overseas assets.

Part of the reason may be the important role played by the investment managers of long standing investment trusts (or closed end funds). These funds, many dating back to the nineteenth century, had a history of involvement in international investment from the railroad expansion in the Americas to the mineral developments in the British Empire and subsequent trading ties. This history of international involvement led fund managers naturally to consider overseas investments when it came to managing large financial resources such as the insurance and pension funds which were expanding fast after the Second World War.

Despite exchange control constraints and the extra premium which often had to be paid to secure investment overseas, most large funds had some exposure and, as the charts in Chapter 9 showed, some had heavy exposure. After 1979 and the relaxation of exchange controls the trend to overseas investments accelerated.

Why should this be? Certainly the returns achieved since that time have not been particularly high relative to returns in the UK (see Table 9.1). To some extent the answer lies in the developments in economic and investment theory which argued that overseas investment provided an efficient means of diversification and hence risk reduction. (Risk in this context being the reduction in short-term volatility of returns.) Certainly these arguments weighed heavily in the USA where investors were bombarded by the arguments for overseas diversification which, they were told, would increase returns and reduce variability!

For UK investors, and for those in the Netherlands, or Switzerland for example, a further argument in favour was the availability of a wider range of investment opportunities which existed compared with their domestic markets. Whatever the reason international investment has grown rapidly across most asset classes but particularly in bonds and equities. This trend added weight to the case for specialist management whether domestically based or based in the region of investment interest.

In the UK these specialist skills often existed already in the investment management houses which played a major role in the investment sector. Thus in many cases the overseas management mandate was wrapped up in the overall balanced mandate – another reason for the slower adoption of specialist fund structures in the UK. Nevertheless there was considerable debate about the benefits of having such overseas assets managed from the home country or from the country or region in which the investments were held. This decision often led to specific portfolios being established therefore and to, at least, some fragmentation of funds into specialist structures.

As with domestic performance the results from overseas investments often fell short of index returns, as shown in Chapter 9. In this case, however, substantially better returns could also materialise. Again the degree of uncertainty was disconcerting for some plan sponsors and the concept of indexation was frequently adopted.

Indexation

The problems associated with manager selection and correct sector allocation has led many funds, particularly in the USA, down the indexed route. What this has meant in practice is that funds have removed some of the uncertainties surrounding performance relative to their chosen benchmark. Having chosen the benchmark the fund sets out to replicate that benchmark within the fund as closely as possible. This can be achieved in one of three major ways.

1. To hold all the constituents in the benchmark index in direct proportion to the index.

2. To use a portfolio optimiser programme to produce a portfolio of stocks which replicates the major characteristics of the benchmark index.

3. To hold a selection of stocks which reflects the sector structure and captures 90% or so of the capitalisation of the benchmark index.

These three methods, replication, optimisation and stratified sampling offer, to varying degrees of accuracy, the same performance as the benchmark. For the fund the advantage is that the achieved return is unlikely to differ markedly from the benchmark index. Most indexed fund managers offer an annualised 'tracking error' of less than 25 basis points for a domestic index fund. That is the indexed fund is likely to deliver a result within 25 basis points of the index in 2 out of 3 years and within 50 basis points roughly 95% of the time. They also offer lower management costs since indexed fees are lower than active manager fees but administration fees can be quite high depending upon the method employed. Figure 10.2 shows the results of UK Equity portfolios relative to the FT–SE Actuaries Index for the years 1986 to 1993. The active and the indexed portfolios are extracted from The WM Company data.

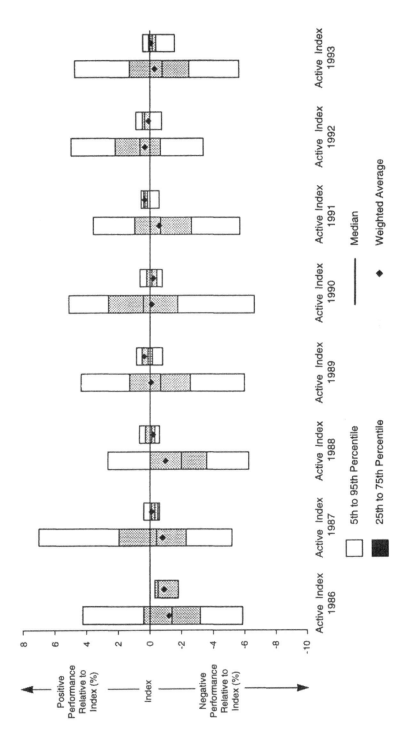

10.2 Range of UK equity returns relative to the FT–SE Actuaries All Share Index.

The much narrower range of returns produced by the sample of indexed funds compared with actively managed funds is apparent. Even so it is clear that some indexed funds exceed the tracking error quoted above. The 5th to 95th percentile range is generally above 1% and sometimes above 2%.

The chart also shows that, in general, the weighted average performance of the indexed or passive funds is higher than the active funds. Over the eight years the indexed funds were 0.1% below the index while the active funds were 0.5% pa below. This differential is usually attributed to the extra costs of activity in actively managed portfolios.

Finally the chart shows a potential drawback/benefit of indexed funds depending on one's perspective. Although the weighted average returns of active managers is below indexed funds, some 40% of active portfolios produce returns above the index. Thus the OPPORTUNITY for superior returns is sacrificed by the indexed funds albeit that the RISK of achieving significantly poor returns is eliminated.

The appeal of indexation was very strong however and by the early 1990s it was estimated that around one-third of US pension funds had their domestic equity exposure indexed and around one-fifth of UK pension funds had their UK equity exposure indexed.

The risks of producing a different performance from expectations due to asset allocation has been tackled in two ways. If the universe was the benchmark, and for many funds in the UK that remains the case, the distribution of assets was kept close to that shown for the universe. Bands around the central asset exposure could be set according to the degree of potential variation which was acceptable to the fund.

The second approach is to set a specific asset allocation benchmark, usually with bands, which is deemed suitable for the fund.

A combination of a constrained asset allocation and indexation within asset classes is an effective way of limiting the variation of achieved returns for the fund compared with the asset class index returns and overall benchmark returns. It cannot, of course, remove the variation in returns from the asset class benchmarks. It is the attitudes to this aspect of uncertainty which lead to the variation in fund structures both within a country and, more evidently, across different countries. These issues are examined in the next chapter.

The issues

A major issue is one which has raged between the investment management profession and the academic community since the sixties. The academic community has claimed that investment returns relative to a market and in any specific asset are random. No persistent management skills can be identified that are statistically significant. That some managers do better than others over any measured period, be it 1 year, 5 years or 10 years is indisputable, as evidenced in the spread of returns shown in Table 10.1 for example. Over succeeding periods, however, the claim is that any superiority in performance will disappear in a random fashion. Evidence for this is examined in Chapter 12. Whatever the truth of the matter, the practical reality is that much of the investment industry pursues its affairs on the assumption that superior performance is attainable and sustainable. Hence, despite the growth in indexation of funds, the bulk of assets are still managed with a view to exceeding an asset benchmark return.

The pursuit of this objective has led to increasingly complex fund structures. A further issue is whether such complexity is justified or could even be self-defeating. Whilst the performance of specific, specialist, portfolios can be measured and relevant benchmarks can be established the question of whether or not the overall fund is achieving satisfactory results becomes more difficult to answer. The complexity often adds to costs, through both activity costs and management charges, and such costs may not be recoverable from superior returns.

If the search for superior asset class returns is an exercise doomed to frustration the variation in returns from different asset classes is a fact which is not disputed. This raises another major issue. If the basic allocation of a fund across asset classes will be the long run determinant of relative returns it is critical that decisions on such allocations be well founded. Many argue that this does not happen. Allocation may be dictated by a desire to follow a peer group even though the specific fund requirements may differ from the peer group. Even where the allocation is specifically determined, by the result of an asset/liability model for example, the input and assumptions in the model may be faulty. Lastly the expected returns on assets may be based on unreliable evidence, perhaps an unusual timespan of historic returns, or an unsuitable definition of risk as discussed in Chapter 8.

11

International differences

Introduction

Not least because of data availability we have so far concentrated our discussion on the experience of UK pension funds. Other funds may need to monitor investment performance but not all are publicly accountable and data is not readily accessible. Investment trusts (closed end funds) and unit trusts (mutual funds) have had their performance monitored over a long period but these tend to be specialist funds. They invest primarily in a single asset class or even in specialist sectors within asset classes. In aggregate their returns are similar to those on the respective assets within pension funds. For example the average fund return tends to fall marginally short of the relevant benchmark index and the range of returns across funds is wide. This can be observed in most of the countries where such funds are available.

For pension funds in other countries different factors come into play. The objectives of the fund can differ from country to country. This chapter examines some of these differences and the effect that they have on the asset structure of funds. In practice these observations are restricted to a comparison of funds in the Netherlands and the USA. Elsewhere in Europe funded pension schemes are not prevalent and where they exist there is, as yet, no structured performance measurement and hence data for comparison.

Pension funds in Europe

For several of the major economies in Europe the pensions, other than state funded schemes, are either on a 'pay as you go' basis as in France, or on a 'book reserve' basis as in Germany and Spain. Although the European Commission drafted a directive on pension funds in 1992 this failed to get ratified, not least

140

Table 11.1 Asset allocation for large pension funds

Country	Domestic Equity	Domestic Bonds	Intl Equity	Intl Bonds	Property	Cash/ Other
Europe						
Belgium	17	35	16	13	8	11
Denmark	14	70	2	0	10	4
Germany	6	75	0	4	15	0
Ireland	32	22	33	2	7	4
Netherlands	7	53	16	5	17	2
Portugal	10	76	1	0	3	10
Switzerland	7	57	3	4	19	10
UK	59	5	24	5	2	1
Sweden *	5	92	0	0	2	15
Finland*	13	47	0	0	25	15
North America						
US*	49	33	3	1	2	12
Canada*	27	48	9	1	7	8
Far East						
Japan*	24	54	5	9	3	5
Hong Kong *	27	3	47	16	0	7
Australia*	39	21	18	6	7	9

Source: MERCER – "European Pension Fund Managers 1993"
* Source: PDFM   - "Pension Fund Indicators"

because of the complexity of pensions practices in the different member states. Company or industry based funded schemes are emerging but are often subject to constraints on their investment freedom.

They are often limited in their application to higher paid workers or as top-ups to state pensions which themselves are often geared to provide much higher pension benefits than prevail in the UK and Netherlands. (Typically 60–70% of national average earnings compared with under 40% in the UK and Netherlands.)   Thus the combination of historic economic and cultural experience with legal and accounting constraints has led to very different fund structures in those countries where private funded pension schemes have developed.

Table 11.1 shows estimated asset allocation of pension funds in those countries where data has been collected. Although the figures may differ from other published sources at the detailed asset level the general picture provided does illustrate the major differences which exist.

Two major areas of difference stand out when we examine the table:

- The range of bond exposure from a low of 10% in the UK to a high of 79% in Germany.

- The range of international exposure from a low of 0% in Sweden and Finland to a high of 47% in Hong Kong.

For the three countries on which reasonable performance data is available – UK, Netherlands and USA – these variations are less extreme but still very marked. The Netherlands and the US experience are examined in more detail below.

The Netherlands experience

The pattern of pension fund liabilities and the experience of investment returns can have an important influence on the way investment funds allocate their assets. When these factors are combined with legal and accounting frameworks which may differ from country to country it is not surprising that the structure of funds can vary when we look at different countries. Table 11.2 shows the end-year asset allocation, by broad category, in the Netherlands for 1988 and 1993. For comparison the figures are derived from universes compiled by The WM Company and differ in detail from the figures shown in Table 11.1. The differences in asset allocation are significant.

The exposure to equities is much lower in the Netherlands although within equities the extent to which overseas shares are held is relatively high. This universe is weighted by the larger funds in the Netherlands which, themselves, have above average equity weightings. For the typical medium to small fund the overall equity exposure was less than 25% at end 1993.

To some extent the low exposure to domestic equities can be accounted for by the limited size of the domestic equity market compared with total pension fund assets. It is estimated that the equities from the Amsterdam Stock Exchange have a total capitalisation little more than half the value of pension

Table 11.2 Netherlands v UK PF asset allocation

		Netherlands P.F. Universe		UK P.F. Universe	
		1988	1993	1988	1993
Equities	Domestic	8	8	53	56
	Overseas	12	21	16	24
Fixed Interest		63	56	14	11
Cash/Other		2	2	6	4
Property/Real Estate		15	13	11	5
Total Assets		100	100	100	100

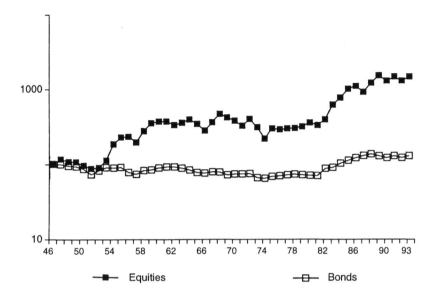

11.1 Total returns on bonds and equities in Netherlands, 1947/91.

fund assets in the Netherlands. Hence the appeal of international equities for pension funds as they seek to broaden their investment universe.

The key difference from the UK experience however is the high exposure to bonds. This is partly explained by the cultural, legal and accounting background in the two countries but also, and importantly by the investment experience. In the Netherlands, for example, accounting practice allowed for bonds to be valued at book or cost while equities had to be valued at market prices. Furthermore funds were often set investment objectives expressed in nominal return terms which could be easily met by the yield on bonds.

Figure 11.1 shows the cumulative real return on domestic equities and bonds in the Netherlands markets. Although equities have significantly outperformed bonds, as they have done in the UK, the outperformance stems from two distinct periods – the 1950s and the 1980s.

Figure 11.2 shows the results for the middle period of the 1960s and 1970s. It was over this period that many of the pension funds were being established and the investment approach was being determined.

Although equities still produced a better return the difference was marginal and three factors were important in assessing the comparative performance over this period.

- Bonds outperformed equities in twelve of the twenty annual periods.

143

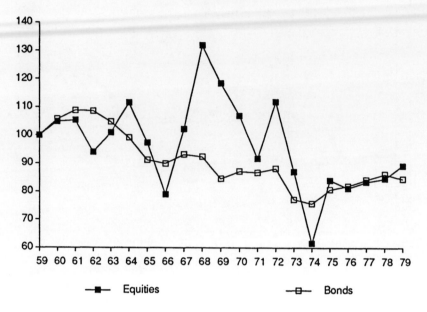

11.2 Cumulative real returns in the 1960s and 1970s.

- Bonds strongly outperformed equities in the seventies.

- Bonds were much less volatile than equities.

With the employees (i.e. the beneficiaries) having a much stronger voice in the structure of the pension funds in the Netherlands compared with the UK (where the employer dominates) it is not surprising that security ranks above costs in their priorities. Despite the long term attractions of equities it is thus understandable that Netherlands pension funds took a different stance on asset allocation than their UK counterparts.

These figures have dealt with index returns, we now look at the returns achieved by a universe of pension funds. Table 11.3 shows the returns of the WM universe of pension funds in the Netherlands for the period 1986-93. The Consumer Price Index (CPI) is also shown to give an indicator of overall real returns.

Over this period the returns from the major asset classes of bonds and equities have been close. Total fixed interest returns of 8.8% pa compared with 9.6% pa for equities, which include international equities. The greater variability of equities is also apparent with annual returns ranging from 42.3% to 18.9% compared with bonds ranging from 16.2% to 1.4%. Despite this experience the trend in asset allocation has been towards a higher equity exposure at the expense of bonds as shown in Table 11.2.

The low inflation rates in the Netherlands have ensured good real returns over the period and in most years, 1990 proving to be an exception. Within the

Table 11.3 Returns by Netherlands pension funds 1986–93

	1986 %	1987 %	1988 %	1989 %	1990 %	1991 %	1992 %	1993 %	8 Year Annualised
Fixed Interest	9.5	6.9	7.5	1.4	4.0	11.4	13.9	16.2	8.8
Private Loans	10.7	6.8	6.7	1.0	3.4	11.0	15.3	13.6	8.5
Guilder Bonds	8.2	7.6	6.9	0.2	4.5	11.1	15.7	17.1	8.9
Intl. Bonds	6.6	4.9	12.0	1.7	2.2	19.5	7.2	22.0	9.3
Equities	8.3	-16.1	33.4	19.8	-18.9	19.2	6.2	42.3	9.6
Cash Other	12.9	15.0	2.1	7.9	9.6	10.8	9.4	14.1	10.1
Real Estate	0.7	3.3	12.7	7.2	3.5	6.6	5.3	10.6	6.2
Total Assets	7.8	1.6	12.4	6.1	-1.3	12.1	10.5	21.7	8.7
CPI	-0.6	-0.2	0.7	1.1	2.5	3.9	3.7	2.1	1.6

universe the range of returns achieved by individual funds is similar to the UK experience.

Table 11.4 shows the 5th and 95th percentile ranges and the inter-quartile ranges for 1993. The 5th– 95th percentile range on total assets is 13.5% while the inter-quartile range is a little under 5%. These are typical of the ranges experienced in the UK (see Chapter 9). Within asset classes the widest range experienced is in real estate but the same caveats on short-term returns data on this asset class apply in the Netherlands as in the UK. The range on equities is wider than in the UK but this data includes international equities which were separately shown for the UK data which would, typically, display a total range of over 20%. Elsewhere the ranges are similar to those experienced in the UK.

Portfolio management risk is therefore an important contributor to the overall uncertainty of returns for Netherlands pension funds. Some of the uncertainty in annual returns is removed over longer time frames, however, as shown in Table 11.5.

Over a 5 year period the inter-quartile range drops to 1% for bonds, 4% for equities and under 5% for real estate. For total assets the overall range is a little over 2% and the inter-quartile range a little over 1%. This compares with the wider ranges in the UK of 4.8% and 1.6% respectively, shown in Table 10.1 (Chapter 10).

Despite a very different asset mix, with much greater exposure to bonds, the experience of Netherlands pension funds bears many similarities to that of UK pension funds. Over the eight years to end 1993 satisfactory real returns were achieved by both universes. In the Netherlands returns on total assets of 8.7% pa compare with a CPI of 1.6% pa. In the UK the equivalent figures were 14.7% pa and 5.0% pa. The rather better experience in the UK owes much to the extra

Table 11.4 1993 range of returns WM Netherlands universe

	95th	75th	25th	5th
Fixed Interest	13.5	14.8	16.9	19.6
Private Loans	10.1	12.5	14.9	17.1
Guilder Bonds	14.3	15.2	17.6	20.8
Intl. Bonds	15.5	17.5	21.5	26.9
Equities	28.0	34.8	43.5	48.3
Real Estate	5.0	10.6	41.6	58.0
Total Assets	16.0	17.9	22.7	29.5

Table 11.5 1989/93 5-year annualised range of returns

	Percentiles				
	95th	75th	25th	5th	Weighted Average
Fixed Interest	8.8	8.9	9.4	9.8	9.2
Private Loans	5.7	8.4	9.3	9.8	8.7
Guilder Bonds	8.7	8.9	9.8	10.4	9.5
Intl. Bonds	8.4	9.2	10.3	20.1	10.2
Equities	6.6	10.0	13.8	14.8	11.9
Real Estate	0.0	2.5	7.2	11.8	6.6
Total Assets	8.1	8.6	9.8	10.3	9.5

weight in, and superior returns from, their domestic equities. Over this period UK Equities returned 16.5% pa to produce an exceptional real return on an asset class representing over 50% of total assets.

The US experience

Performance data on funds in the USA have been available for longer than in most countries. Mutual fund data has been the source of much academic research since the 1960s and pension fund data became available at that time. Given the scale of the business, however, the number and type of universes has proliferated. Unlike the UK where two organisations account for the bulk of pension funds subject to performance measurement there are many such organisations in the US. Performance data is often produced by the management organisation and submitted for inclusion in a universe in contrast to UK practice where the performance is calculated by the provider of the universe data. This absence of independently produced data across the industry has led to much greater variation in calculation and presentational standards in the USA. In addressing this problem the AIMR produced a detailed documentation of standards to be adopted if performance data was to be used for advertising, or promotional purposes or was to be included in peer group universes. (See Chapter 7.)

The data used in this chapter is therefore a less comprehensive sample of pension funds in the US than the equivalent data used for the UK or Netherlands. Nevertheless it presents a valid indication of the US experience and reflects the different characteristics of the pension fund business in the USA.

Asset allocation

The provision of retirement pensions by the private sector through funded arrangements has been widespread in the USA. The majority of schemes are of the defined benefit type although defined contribution schemes are also popular. Of the defined benefit schemes many do not offer direct salary related benefits but are defined in terms of nominal retirement income (e.g. $2000 per month), with or without inflation upgrades. Thus the extent to which funds are exposed to inflation risk can vary widely. This, combined with the returns experienced on different asset categories, has led to a variety of asset allocation strategies. Within a typical universe of funds for example the range of equity exposure in 1993 was 83% to 0% and the range of bond exposure was similarly wide at 71% to ½%. This contrasts with a universe of UK pension funds where the domestic equity range, although wide, showed the 95th percentile fund still having 47% exposure to UK equities. (See Fig. 9.2.)

Despite the existence of such a wide variety of pension fund structures the aggregate distribution of pension funds in the US reflects the basic characteristics of the sector and the investment returns experienced. Table 11.6 shows the estimated aggregate pension fund asset distribution in the USA with the Netherlands and UK shown for comparison.

The much lower international exposure of US funds is the first feature to stand out. Nevertheless the overall scale of US funds means that the absolute impact of their international investment on non-US markets can be significant. Total international assets are roughly similar in value to those of the UK pension fund sector despite the much lower proportion shown in the table. The equity/bond split of US funds falls between the high bond exposure of the Netherlands and the low bond exposure of the UK.

As mentioned earlier, however, the US pension fund sector covers a particularly wide range of funds having very diverse, liability profiles and hence asset allocation strategies. Accounting conventions have also played their part in

Table 11.6 Estimated pension fund asset distribution 1993

Asset	Netherlands	US	UK
Domestic	57	81	63
Equities	8	44	56
Bonds	49	37	7
International	28	8	28
Equities	21	6	24
Bonds	7	2	4
Other	15	11	9

Table 11.7 Master Trust universe results

	1 Year	5 Years	10 Years
5th Percentile	2.8	10.4	14.0
25th Percentile	0.5	9.2	12.7
50th Percentile	-0.8	8.4	12.0
75th Percentile	-2.1	7.7	11.1
95th Percentile	-3.8	6.8	10.0

Source: Bankers Trust – Master Trust Universe

influencing funds towards bond exposure since annual book profits/losses must be taken into consideration in the company accounts.

Total returns of US pension funds

As mentioned earlier a comprehensive universe of pension funds is less easy to find in the US with several performance measurers maintaining universes. The earliest available universe was that developed by A G Becker, subsequently to become the SEI Corporation. They produced a series of linked median fund returns from 1963 onwards. Over the period 1970–1984 the SEI Linked Median Large Plan produced an annualised return of 7.1%. This compares with a passive 60/40 US Stocks/Bonds mix return of 9.3% and a return on the First Chicago Investment Advisors MMI of 10.4%.

Table 11.7 shows the results of the Bankers Trust, Master Trust Universe for periods ending December 1994. The range of returns over the ten year period at 4% compares with those shown for UK funds at 3.9% (Table 10.1). The 1 year and 5 year ranges are lower than the equivalent figures for UK funds.

Overall the returns experience is more notable for the similarities with other countries than for the differences. The narrower overall range of returns may be due to the higher proportion of funds which are indexed than to any less diversity in the returns produced by active managers.

Conclusion

Although the different environments against which pension funds operate in the different countries has led to different fund structures the underlying investment returns are similar. Funds tend to produce returns in aggregate below the relevant index benchmarks which can be largely attributed to the expenses of management.

Returns within asset classes vary widely but by similar amounts in the different countries. Thus despite their differences funds face very similar problems in seeking the optimum asset structure to meet their liabilities. Their search for superior performance is also fraught with the same difficulties of fund structure and manager selection.

The issues

That the structure of pension funds differs to such a degree across countries can only partially be attributed to different investment experience. Should funds be pushed towards a common pattern of asset allocation therefore?

In striving to impose common standards and common responses to investment returns the investment management profession must be conscious of the cultural, legal and accounting differences which exist. What works in the USA may not work in the UK and what works in both may not work in Japan or in Continental Europe.

International comparisons may be interesting but it would be dangerous to use the experience in one market to influence the practice in another, some aspects of which are discussed in Chapter 12.

Myths and misunderstandings

Introduction

There are often commonly accepted views about investment returns which may not stand the test of experience or may not apply in different markets. Thus much of the academic work in the investment field emanated from the USA and was developed on the basis of US experience. The economic environment in the USA for the past seventy years and its impact on corporate profits, interest rates, inflation and exchange rates, all key variables affecting investment markets, has been very different from that experienced in the UK or other European markets for example.

Moreover many of our accepted wisdoms about asset returns have been based on indices constructed to represent a market experience. Some indices do this better than others but none of them reflect the experience of 'live' funds. For example, the experience of a broad universe of equity funds is that they will underperform an index over time because they are incurring real running and transaction costs. This is less of a problem with bonds so that bond portfolios will not suffer the same shortfall against a market index. Thus the apparent advantage that equities have over bonds in terms of superior long term returns may be less than is indicated by index results.

With performance measurement of a substantial universe of funds having been carried out in the UK for some twenty years a useful body of data is now available to test some of these assumptions against real life experience. The WM Company have conducted various tests on their data in order to throw some light on issues of interest to investors. Some of the results confirm existing wisdom, albeit with modifications, while others provide conflicting evidence. These extracts from research carried out at The WM Company provide interesting examples of how our knowledge and understanding of the investment management process can be helped by performance measurement and analysis applied consistently over a number of years.

Asset class returns

To illustrate the difference between asset class returns achieved by funds compared with market indices, Table 12.1 shows the annualised returns for the WM universe of UK pension funds for the years 1977–93 in UK equities, overseas equities and UK bonds. Also shown are the returns calculated for representative indices for these asset classes which might, typically, be quoted to illustrate asset class returns.

When looking at the index experience UK equities have comfortably outperformed UK bonds while overseas equities have marginally outperformed UK bonds. Actual fund experience has been different, however, with the gap between UK equities and bonds narrowing from almost 7% pa to under 5% pa. Returns from UK bonds have actually exceeded returns achieved on overseas equities by 2½% pa compared with a shortfall of almost 1% pa on the index data.

That funds have outperformed the bond index is as much to do with the fact that broad bond indices of the type represented by the FT–Actuaries All Stocks Index used here, are not satisfactory benchmarks for typical pension fund bond portfolios, as it is to do with particular management skills. Nevertheless such indices are often quoted when comparing the attractions of equities versus bonds based on historic returns.

Table 12.1 Asset class returns 1977/93

Annualised Returns for Period	UK Equities		Overseas Equities		UK Bonds	
	WM	Index	WM	Index	WM	Index
1977/93	20.3	21.0	13.1	15.0	15.6	14.1

Small funds outperform large funds

Another popular concept has been that smaller funds, because of their ability to be more flexible and to trade closer to market size, should produce superior performance. Here the evidence is mixed since at the total fund level it does appear that small funds outperform their larger brethren. For example Table 12.2 shows the ten year annualised results for the WM universe for the years 1984–93.

Although small funds have produced better returns on total assets than the very large funds in the sample this result clearly owes more to the mix of assets than to the returns within asset classes. The relatively poor returns on UK

Table 12.2 WM universe results by size band

	Very Small £m0-5	Small £m5-15	Medium £m15-100	Large £m100-1000	Very Large £m>1000
UK Equities	17.7	18.0	17.9	17.9	18.2
Overseas Equities	13.5	13.8	14.0	13.7	14.9
UK Bonds	12.7	13.2	13.3	13.5	13.8
Total (ex Property)	15.4	15.8	15.8	15.8	16.0
UK Property	-	8.2	8.4	9.5	9.6
Total Assets	15.2	15.6	15.6	15.4	15.0

Source: The WM Company – Annual Review UK Pension Fund Service

property hold the clue to this outcome since the large and very large funds have held much higher proportions of property than the smaller funds. Significantly the results within asset classes show, if anything, that very large funds have achieved better returns over this period although there is little to choose between funds in the small to large range.

Fast growth leads to better performance

The rationale behind this concept is that a high net inflow of cash allows a fund to be more flexible, allowing it to adjust asset allocation without incurring switching costs. A potential drawback, until the more recent access to index futures, was that high cash flow could not always be invested rapidly enough in fast rising markets. An analysis of the WM pension fund universe over the ten year period 1984–93 in fact shows no evidence of a correlation between growth and fund performance.

Table 12.3 shows the annual returns for the universe and for groups of funds classified in each year by the proportion of net new money available. Funds which experienced rapid growth in net new money (>20%) outperformed the WM universe average in five of the ten years and interestingly, in years of strong as well as weak market performance.

The group with the best record of outperformance has been where net new money has been under 5% of fund value. This group outperformed in eight of the ten years but the variation from the average has only twice exceeded ½% – in 1984 and 1986 – in contrast to the volatility of the fast growth group.

Funds showing negative growth show the fewest years of outperformance. Such funds may hold a different asset mix to the average with a tendency to hold more bonds to reflect a greater maturity of liabilities. In general, however, there is no obvious difference in asset allocation between the groups classified by net

Table 12.3 WM universe returns 1984/93 by growth rate

% Net New Growth	% Returns (including Property)									
	1984	1985	1986	1987	1988	1989	1990	1991	1992	1993
< 20	19.7	15.9	24.9	1.7	11.7	32.7	-10.3	16.7	19.1	29.2
11-20	20.1	15.8	24.5	3.0	13.9	30.3	-10.7	16.4	20.2	28.7
6-10	20.2	14.2	22.1	4.6	13.9	30.2	-10.7	18.0	18.5	28.5
0-5	20.9	14.9	23.2	3.5	14.2	30.3	-10.5	16.8	18.7	28.4
Negative	20.2	16.0	23.3	2.1	13.0	31.2	-11.1	16.5	18.5	28.0
WM Universe	20.3	14.5	22.5	3.4	13.8	30.3	-10.6	16.9	18.6	28.2

Source: The WM Company – Annual Review UK Pension Fund Service

new money growth, nor is there evidence of performance differences on a consistent basis.

Local management is better than foreign based management

The logic behind this statement is that local management have greater knowledge of their own markets, better market contacts, superior information and faster response times than managers based in another country.

When testing the validity of the statement considerable care must be taken to ensure that fair comparisons are being made. For example a comparison of the returns on UK Equities achieved by a universe of UK pension funds and a universe of US pension funds shows that the UK pension funds achieved superior returns. Superficially the UK domestic managers did better than their US counterparts in the UK equity market as shown in Fig. 12.1. Several points need to be made:

- Within each universe the domicile of the manager is not clarified, although most of the UK universe will have UK based managers the US universe may have managers based in the US, UK or other countries.

- The universes are of an entirely different scale. The UK was valued at end period at £151.7bn, representing over 50% of fund assets, the US universe was valued at £1.2bn representing less than 1% of underlying fund assets.

- The average number of holdings per portfolio for the UK universe was close to 100 while for the US universe it was less than 20.

- The average level of activity for the UK universe was around half that for the US universe, thus incurring lower costs.

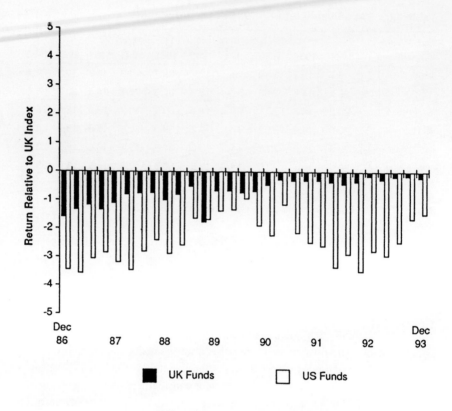

12.1 UK and US funds relative performance in UK equities.

In Fig. 12.2 the last three year period 1990–92 is shown using the US universe only. In this instance the domicile of the managers within this universe has been clarified with US based and UK based managers separately identified. The cumulative results of each sub-universe is plotted with the quarterly performance of the UK based managers relative to the US based managers also shown (RHS).

Over the three years the UK based managers have shown the better performance with a return of 5.0% pa versus 3.2% pa for the US based managers. The quarterly pattern is not consistent however, with five of the twelve quarters showing poorer returns from UK based managers. Nevertheless on this, limited, evidence the domestically based managers have shown the better returns. Interestingly, for the same sample of managers, the US based managers reversed the result when the overall returns for the EAFE Index are examined.

If we examine the results of a broad universe of US pension funds in their domestic market they show higher returns than a universe of UK pension funds achieved from US equities; both results in US dollars. This is shown in Fig. 12.3. Once again similar comments can be made as in Fig. 12.1.

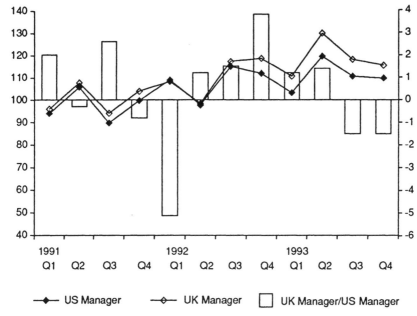

12.2 US v UK manager returns in UK equities.

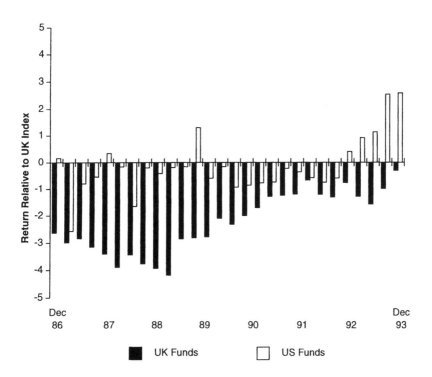

12.3 UK and US funds relative return in US equities.

Although the limited evidence thus supports the opening statement it is by no means overwhelming and care must be taken when assessing results to ensure that they represent fair comparisons.

Combining overseas with domestic equities raises returns and reduces risk

This was a popular contention promoted by commentators in the USA to promote and encourage US funds to invest overseas. In the early seventies Bruno Solnik presented a paper – 'Why Diversify Internationally?' – which gave a sound academic basis for international diversification. The correlation coefficients of equity returns from different markets were always less than 1. For a US based investor indeed the correlation coefficient with other major markets never exceeded .75. Although the volatility of some of these markets exceeded that of the US market the effect of combining the two was to produce a volatility lower than either – such was the effect of less than perfect correlation.

The enactment of the Employee Retirement Income Security Act (ERISA) in 1974 opened the way for pension funds to invest in broadly diversified overseas portfolios without fear of breaching the 'prudent man rules'. Prior to the act each individual holding had to be justified on the basis that a prudent man would feel comfortable investing in it. A highly volatile foreign stock about which imperfect information was available would probably have fallen foul of this criterion. Under ERISA it became acceptable to invest if it could be shown that the effect on the overall portfolio was beneficial. In this context a reduction in portfolio volatility was regarded as beneficial.

Additionally it could be demonstrated that the returns from overseas markets were actually higher than those on the US. Table 12.4 shows the US dollar returns over the period 1969–88 for the US, Japan, UK and the MSCI World Index (ex US).

The correlation coefficient between the US and the world (ex-US) typically emerges at under .5 so it could be demonstrated that combining international

Table 12.4 Annualised equity returns (US$) 1969/88

	1969/88 %	Standard Deviation %
USA	9.52	17.82
Japan	18.07	29.35
UK	13.28	37.86
World (ex USA)	15.77	22.19

equities with US equities not only increased returns over this period but also reduced volatility compared with a 100% US equity portfolio. Whilst the returns achieved are likely to vary from period to period the correlations remain more stable. Internationalisation of investment may bring markets more closely into line but this is a slow process and they are never likely to achieve total correlation. The experience of international investment from the US is not, necessarily, repeated for UK or European based investors.

Figures 12.4 and 12.5 show the experience of UK pension funds over the years 1983–92. Between 21% and 29% of equities were invested overseas by UK based pension funds during this period. Figure 12.4 shows the rolling three year annualised returns for periods ending December 1985 through to December 1992. The two lines represent the UK equity returns and the composite equity portfolio returns. Only in the earlier years did the overseas content add to the UK returns. For most periods since those ending in December 1986 the composite portfolio has produced lower returns than UK equities alone.

Figure 12.5 shows the annualised variability of the two samples. In this case the variability of the composite portfolio is consistently lower than the UK equity portfolio. For UK investors therefore only half of the original contention can be said to hold. International equities reduce risk (volatility) when combined with domestic equities but have a variable impact on returns.

For some European Continental investors even the reduction in volatility can fail to materialise. The data shown in Fig. 12.6 is that from the viewpoint of a Netherlands based investor. A portfolio comprising 90% Netherlands equities and 10% world (ex-Netherlands) equities is shown relative to 100% Netherlands equities. Rolling 3 year annualised returns are used for periods ending December 1983 to December 1993. Except for a few periods ending March 1987 through to December 1989 the composite portfolio underperformed Netherlands equities. Overseas diversification rarely added value to domestic equity returns.

The chart also plots the difference in the standard deviation of the composite portfolio and domestic equities. These results are more surprising. For periods up to end 1990 the variability conformed to expectations; the composite portfolio had lower variability than domestic equities. For the later periods however the reverse has occurred and the incorporation of 10% overseas equities into the portfolio had the effect of increasing volatility overall. Thus for those periods ending between December 1990 and June 1993 an internationally diversified portfolio for a Netherlands investor provided lower returns and higher volatility!

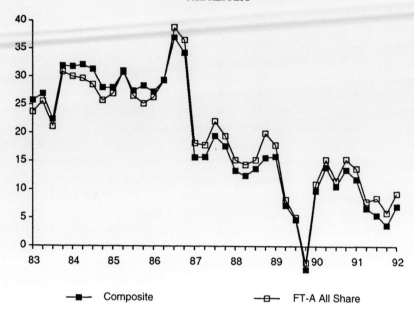

12.4 Annualised return – composite v index.

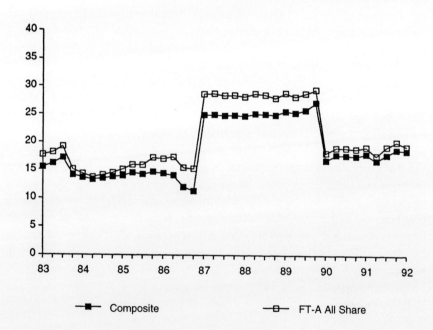

12.5 Annualised variability – composite v index.

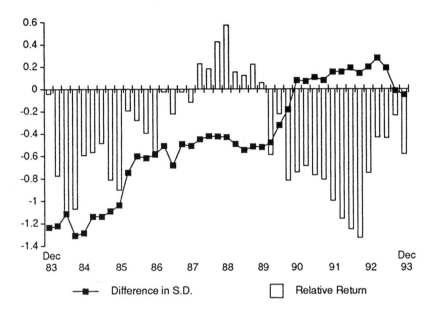

12.6 Netherlands composite portfolio relative to Netherlands equities.

Superior investment returns are sustainable

Investors retain great faith in the concept that investment skill produces superior results and that such skill is sustainable over time. Academics, by contrast, have presented arguments to the effect that returns from investments, in broadly efficient markets, are random and investment skills cannot ensure sustained superior results.

The arguments range to and fro with asset managers showing evidence of portfolios with a strong record of beating their benchmark. The academics have countered that most such runs of good returns can be shown to be statistically random – a lifetime is needed to refute the random contention. Table 12.5 shows the results from the analysis of a sample of UK pension funds over a seven year period 1986–92.

Some 409 funds were analysed and the table shows the incidence of top quartile performance over the seven years. The figures in bold show results which were significantly higher than random at the 95% confidence level. Italics show a statistically significant lower result. The risk adjusted figures take account of distinct market phases. Although showing marginal evidence that some funds showed consistency of good performance this still meant that only 3% of funds in the sample achieved top quartile performance in at least five of the seven years. Moreover there was little predictability; the performance of a fund from one period to the next could not be forecast accurately. Similar

Table 12.5 Numbers of funds in top quartile: actual v random

Possible Times in Top Quartile	7	6	5	4	3	2	1	0
Expected (Random)	0	1	5	24	71	127	127	55
Actual	0	2	10	28	60	114	139	56
Actual (Risk Adj.)	0	4	9	32	65	*95*	139	65

Table 12.6 Erosion of top quartile status of UK equity portfolios

	Initial Period	Percentage of Funds Retaining Top - Quartile Status -						
	1983/ 1985	1984/ 1986	1985/ 1987	1986/ 1988	1987/ 1989	1988/ 1990	1989/ 1991	1990/ 1992
Percentage of Top Quartile Funds in Initial Period	100	63	38	27	22	14	10	4
Random Outcome	100			25			6¼	

analysis on specific asset portfolios shows similar, limited, variation of results from a random outturn.

Table 12.6 shows the erosion of top quartile status of a sample of UK equity portfolios within UK pension funds. Rolling three year returns are used to smooth out short-term aberrations. Again the actual outcome is slightly better than random indicating some marginal statistical significance in favour of consistency. Nevertheless by the end of the period the results are very close to random and only 1% of the original universe achieved top quartile performance and sustained it. Selecting that 1% remains a major problem for investors seeking superior management skills! Apart from its implications for evidence of consistency these results throw light on the extent to which funds which target top quartile performance for their managers are doomed to disappointment.

The issues

Assertions and claims made by investment professionals and academics alike need very careful analysis. Many claims from either side are made on the basis of index or market price data. Periods are often chosen to suit the argument and the quality of the analysis can, and is, often questioned. For preference such claims should be based on actual results, independently verified, of live funds. Despite the existence of performance measurement for over a quarter of a century, long term relevant data remains hard to come by. Thus even the examples cited in this chapter are based on relatively limited data over comparatively short time periods. For every example shown it is possible that a different sample, from a different country over a different time frame will produce contradictory results.

Statistical analysis of historic data can be helpful and informative but it needs treating with especial care and a degree of scepticism. The application of common sense is essential.

SECTION

The future

This final section looks to the future and assesses the likely developments in performance measurement based on recent trends. Chapter 13 assesses the trend towards more detailed analysis. The advent of global markets, internationally invested funds and the speed of electronic transmission and processing of data is likely to facilitate more detailed analysis and more accurate and comparable information.

The evolution of pension funds in countries where they are not yet well established and the increasing maturity of funds where they already are established will lead to more diverse universes of funds. These trends and their implications are discussed in Chapter 14.

Chapter 15 looks at the impact of these developments on the demand for improved standards. In particular the growth in international investment and the trend towards global funds for trans-national corporations will require the establishment of internationally accepted standards. But social and cultural differences as well as differing accounting and legal frameworks may make this difficult.

More detailed analysis

Introduction

Just as the evolution of portfolio theory has been facilitated by the availability of data and of faster, cheaper processing capabilities so too will the performance measurement process be enhanced. For those recipients of encyclopaedia size reports on their fund the thought of more detailed analysis will be greeted with dismay.

Why should we want more detail? More is not always better.

The general climate for disclosure and accountability is becoming more and more demanding, however, and performance measurement is an integral part of that process. Fiduciaries at all levels not only have to carry out their responsibilities thoroughly, but they must also be seen to have done so at all stages and up to specified standards of performance. In this chapter we speculate on where such developments might take us.

Stock level transaction data

With the increasing use of electronic market systems, reporting mechanisms and recording methods it will become relatively straightforward to gather portfolio and fund data at the transaction point. This has several advantages for the fund manager in so far as he is able to access up to the minute information on the fund, its value, structure and performance. In the fund performance measurement context it should improve the accuracy with which time weighted returns can be calculated, for example. If the performance measurer has access to the same detail of data there will no longer be the need to estimate cash flows within the fund, they can be accurately day or even time recorded.

Moreover if the performance measurer has similar access to all the funds within their particular universe, fast and accurate aggregate data can be calculated and comparative performance information can be made available in a timely fashion. This can be of considerable value to the fund manager seeking to perform against a peer group benchmark. For the plan sponsor too the speedier availability of reports may be of value although with a longer management timescale for most practical decisions this is less relevant. Of greater benefit to the plan sponsor is the potential to monitor and assess the performance of the manager and the overall way in which the fund is managed. The efficiency with which trades are executed, the costs incurred and the impact on the overall portfolio of such transactions can all be measured. Already there are services which measure not just the overall performance of the fund but the efficiency with which specific trades are executed.

Monitoring foreign exchange trades

For example the rate at which foreign exchange transactions are completed is being compared with market averages and closing levels. This analysis enables the plan sponsor to assess the efficiency of the process in achieving attractive exchange rates.

Table 13.1 shows an extract from a foreign exchange transaction report. Its purpose is to record all foreign exchange transactions carried out by a specific executor (which need not always be the portfolio manager but might be the custodian for example). The actual trade rate is compared with the market rates over the day and the mid-market rate and deviations are calculated.

These are then summarised for the portfolio over a specified period and categorised by transaction size. An example is shown in Table 13.2. An overall fund summary can be produced if there is more than one portfolio or executor. Table 13.2 calculates the financial impact on the portfolio of all the transactions relative to the assumption that all deals were completed at mid-market price. Thus the efficiency of the executor of the deal can be monitored and any unusual transactions identified.

Monitoring efficiency of execution

The availability of stock level transaction data will enable similar analysis to be carried out to assess the efficiency with which managers implement their investment decisions. If the data is analysed by the brokers used by the manager, the relative costs and effectiveness of each broker can be monitored, providing an automatic audit on the relationship between manager and broker.

Table 13.3 shows an example of such a monitoring process already in use in the USA where detailed market data is available on a timely and accessible basis. Section A of the table shows summary data for each manager indicating total commission generated, commission per share, execution cost per share (defined

Table 13.1 Sample foreign exchange analysis transaction report

01 Oct 93 to 31 Dec 93				TRANSACTION REPORT					Demonstration Client	
Trade Date	Forward Settlement Date	Sell From	By To	Trade Rate	Market Best	Market Low	Basis Points Range From	% Deal From Mid Mid	Transaction Value (GBP)	Transaction Sizeband
Portfolio :	Portfolio 1									
Manager :	Manager 1									
Mandate:	Balanced									
Executor :	Executor 1									
05 Oct 93	12 Oct 93	3,467,201 DEM	1,409,431 GBP	0.406504	0.407847	0.404727	38	14	1,409,431	C
05 Oct 93	12 Oct 93	1,395,814 NLG	505,181 GBP	0.361925	0.362856	0.360501	33	21	506,181	B
06 Oct 93	12 Oct 93	412,329 AUD	176,586 GBP	0.428266	0.436063	0.425941	117	(54)	176,586	B
07 Oct 93	13 Oct 93	327,843 NLG	117,870 GBP	0.359531	0.360403	0.358658	24	0	117,870	A
07 Oct 93	13 Oct 93	1,737,890 NLG	6224,826 GBP	0.359531	0.360403	0.358658	24	0	624,826	B
08 Oct 93		1,946,055 NLG	224,718 GBP	0.115473	0.115930	0.115144	34	(16)	224,718	B
08 Oct 93		152,055 FRF	8,137,993 BEF	53.519998	53.914100	53.309600	56	(30)	152,055	A
08 Oct 93		1,323,492 GBP	13,211,631 DKK	9.982400	10.054400	9.954300	50	(44)	1,323,492	C
08 Oct 93	13 Oct 93	407,539 AUD	174,786 GBP	0.428881	0.430730	0.426523	49	12	174,786	B
08 Oct 93	13 Oct 93	859,057 GBP	45,976,720 BEF	53.520000	53.919544	53.314983	56	(32)	589,057	C
08 Oct 93	14 Oct 93	599,480 AUD	257,106 GBP	0.428881	0.430742	0.426535	49	12	257,106	B
08 Oct 93	14 Oct 93	195,808 NLG	70,556 GBP	0.360334	0.361943	0.358530	47	6	70,556	A
11 Oct 93		1,763,144 GBP	17,534,808 DKK	9.950300	9.985900	9.897000	45	20	1,763,144	C
11 Oct 93	15 Oct 93	133,455 AUD	48,547 GBP	0.427899	0.432888	0.427156	67	(74)	48,547	A
11 Oct 93	15 Oct 93	508,515 DEM	206,755 GBP	0.406587	0.407889	0.405754	26	(22)	206,755	B
11 Oct 93	15 Oct 93	196,200 NLG	70,923 GBP	0.361481	0.362328	0.360642	23	0	70,923	A
11 Oct 93	15 Oct 93	917,668 USD	596,741 GBP	0.650280	0.654119	0.649447	36	(64)	596,741	B
12 Oct 93	15 Oct 93	722,260 GBP	8,760,000 SEK	12.128600	12.219500	12.076992	59	(28)	722,260	C
12 Oct 93	18 Oct 93	612,784 USD	400,251 GBP	0.653168	0.655283	0.650594	36	10	400,251	B
12 Oct 93	19 Oct 93	905,153 USD	589,869 GBP	0.651678	0.655330	0.650641	36	(56)	589,869	B
13 Oct 93		2,931,940 FRF	341,169 GBP	0.116363	0.116919	0.115789	49	2	341,169	B
13 Oct 93	19 Oct 93	1,248,226 AUD	538,771 GBP	0.431630	0.436251	0.429968	73	(47)	538,771	B

Table 13.2 Sample foreign exchange transaction summary

01 Oct 93 to 31 Dec 93			TRANSACTION REPORT					Demonstration Client	
Portfolio	Executor	Transaction Sizeband	Total Number of Transactions	Basis Points Range From	% Deal From Mid	Basis Points From Mid	Transaction Value (GBP)	Financial Impact (GBP)	
Portfolio 1	Executor 1	A	66	50	(24)	(12)	5,715,199	(6,741)	
		B	98	44	(19)	(8)	36,156,434	(29,583)	
		C	42	42	(17)	(7)	64,415,982	(45,368)	
		All	206	-	-	(8)	106,287,615	(81,693)	
Overall Summary			206	-	-	(8)	106,287,615	(81,693)	

Table 13.3 Sample stock transaction analysis US equities by manager

Section A

Manager	Total Brokerage Commission	Commission Cost Per Share	Execution Cost Per Share	Total Cost Turnover	Portfolio	Trades Outside Range	Percentage of Purchases at or Below VWA	Percentage of Sales at or Above VWA
Manager A	19,845.00	0.024	0.015	0.040	46.47	6	32.10%	53.33
Manager B	32,453.00	0.028	-0.079	-0.051	51.91	4	51.61%	43.48
Manager C	66,836.00	0.027	0.046	0.073	48.91	1	36.89%	40.00
Manager D	11,418.00	0.033	0.035	0.068	3.29	3	38.46%	50.00
Manager E	23,400.00	0.043	0.000	0.043	7.17	0	52.38%	44.00
Manager F	93,909.50	0.038	0.094	0.131	65.25	3	38.99%	31.82
Manager G	47,654.60	0.026	-0.045	-0.019	36.39	6	66.02%	46.94
Manager H	19,234.80	0.056	0.132	0.188	10.57	1	57.69%	67.65
Manager I	21,847.00	0.021	-0.057	-0.036	121.43	3	25.00%	58.93
	336,598.00	0.030	0.016	0.047	11.31	27	44.73%	48.57%
BT Universe	1,992,752.00	0.041	0.109	0.150	0.05	98	48.09%	42.36%

Source: Bankers Trust Company

Table 13.3 continued

Section B									
	Trades	Shares	Principal	Shares Per Trade	Commission Per Trade	Comm Cost Cents Per Share	Comm Cost % of Principal	Exec Cost Cents Per Share	Exec Cost % of Principal
Manager A	171	818,800	35,423,045	4,788	116	2.42	0.06%	1.55	0.04%
Manager B	54	1,171,800	56,518,513	21,700	601	2.77	0.06%	-7.86	-0.16%
Manager C	173	2,479,700	90,528,622	14,334	386	2.70	0.07%	4.61	0.13%
Manager D	25	343,200	10,460,412	13,728	457	3.33	0.11%	3.50	0.11%
Manager E	46	550,000	23,204,198	11,957	509	4.25	0.10%	0.01	0.00%
Manager F	269	2,482,700	115,879,171	9,229	349	3.78	0.08%	9.36	0.20%
Manager G	201	1,857,370	61,038,852	9,241	237	2.57	0.08%	-4.48	-0.14%
Manager H	60	342,422	16,319,688	5,707	321	5.62	0.12%	13.17	0.28%
Manager I	172	1,040,400	52,258,957	6,049	127	2.10	0.04%	-5.75	-0.11%
	1,171	11,086,392	461,631,457	9,467	287	3.04	0.07%	1.64	0.04%
BT Universe	5,707	48,463,975	1,747,235,063	8,492	349	4.11	0.11%	10.89	0.30%

Source: Bankers Trust Company

as the difference between achieved price and the volume weighted average price on the day – VWA) and hence total cost per share, relative to an average market transaction on that day. The final two columns show the percentage purchases or sales made at VWA prices or better. Section B in the table continues the analysis on a per trade basis to establish the overall cost per trade as a percent of principal. The bottom line shows the figures for a universe of funds as a benchmark.

Similar analysis is carried out at the broker account level to generate information on the cost and efficiency of the execution brokers used by the fund.

Both of these analyses depend upon the easy availability of transaction level data not only for the specific fund but also for the overall market in order that meaningful comparisons can be made. As more markets move to electronic dealing and reporting, such data will become more commonplace.

What are the benefits?

How relevant is such detailed analysis to the plan sponsor and the overall performance measurement of the fund? It might be argued that the costs being analysed in these examples are immaterial relative to the ultimate success of the investment decisions underlying these transactions. In the broadest terms this is likely to be the case and successful investment decisions will outweigh such considerations.

Nevertheless there are valid reasons for wanting such detailed information and the analysis which can be extracted from it.

- Even successful decisions could produce better results if they are executed more efficiently.

- The availability and analysis of the detailed data provides an audit on the operations of all concerned with the fund – aberrations can be investigated.

- More detailed information allows more informed judgement on the source of performance – good or bad – and the likelihood of its continuing.

- If investment performance, in the long run, can be expected to be no better than average then containing costs may be the key factor in the fund's overall relative return.

- Where there is little to choose between managers the record of execution efficiency may be a critical factor. For example in Table 13.3 Manager 4 appears to incur consistently above average costs despite the fact that execution prices on average are better than the VWA. Is he using brokers with higher charges or getting poorer service from his brokers?

171

These are relatively new areas for analysis based on greater availability of data. Existing areas of analysis of overall returns as described in Chapter 3 are also likely to benefit from fast access to detailed data.

More accurate attribution

Within equity portfolios the trend towards more detailed performance attribution is already well established. Easier access to data will allow effective stock level attribution to be calculated covering both basic stock selection and the impact of timing.

Performance analysis is already moving away from the established asset/sector/stock classification of portfolios. Disection of the portfolio by stock characteristics, either style analysis or factor analysis is commonplace in the US and performance attribution along these lines is likely to develop further. It is imperative, however, that the attribution analysis reflects the management process and is not simply imposed as a fashionable tool.

New investment instruments

A major challenge facing the performance measurers currently is to cope adequately with new instruments and portfolio management techniques. In Chapter 5, we examined the models for relative attribution in use commonly but more complex management techniques will demand more complex performance models. Currency hedging, options strategies, with their increasing complexity, and the more frequent use of futures, TAA overlays, currency overlays, etc, will demand performance measurement tools to match.

A recent example will illustrate the complexities now confronting performance measurers. Figure 13.1 shows the US$ exposure of an international bond fund and of its benchmark index. Also shown is the exchange rate of the dollar against the Deutschmark and the yen. The fund has six bond managers and Fig. 13.2 shows the US$ exposure of each of the managers. The variation in exposure from the benchmark may be due to different proportions of dollar bonds relative to the benchmark or to taking long or short positions in the currency relative to the underlying bond exposure.

The currency positions can be achieved by forward contracts, futures or options. The challenge for the performance measurer in this case is to calculate the contribution to the relative performance of the fund from each of the managers and attribute this to its component parts – bond market selection, bond selection within markets and currency.

Bearing in mind that such portfolios are likely to be very actively managed with security and currency positions changing daily, even intra-daily, and in substantial proportions, the need for detailed and timely data becomes obvious.

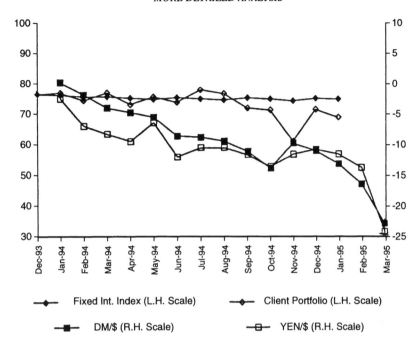

13.1 Currency exposure and exchange rate.

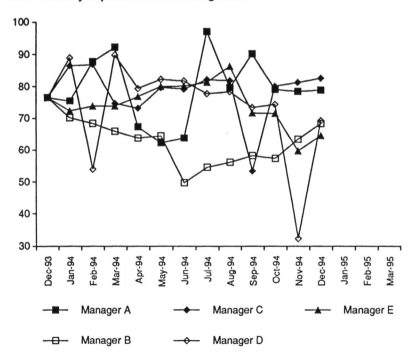

13.2 Dollar exposure by manager.

The issues

There is a danger that clients will be inundated with data but, if so, the fault will ultimately lie with the quality of the analysis rather than the availability of the data. Good management information relies on the availability of timely and detailed data but the management need not see the detail. What is required is effective analysis of the data to produce meaningful reports.

This is where the competition in performance measurement and analysis will emerge. The development of more effective systems will allow the production of more timely and relevant management reports. Detailed transaction level data of itself could cloud the issue but it is the raw material for effective statistical analysis which should provide useful management reports.

It is argued that the performance measurers are chasing data for its own sake – data mining. It is certainly true that availability of fresh data leads to an outbreak of analysis – often by the academic community in the first instance. But unless the analysis produces something of interest or value it is unlikely to be adopted by commercial organisations. Furthermore even analysis which has no immediate commercial value can add to the long run understanding of how markets work. By its nature research involves much work which is not cost effective but can ultimately produce something of value. The availability of 'live' transaction data may eventually lead to modifications in portfolio theory, much of which has been built up on the basis of crude market indicated prices.

This raises a further issue – is it cost effective? In general, commercial disciplines will ensure that it is. The desirability of more detailed data is not new but only the advent of cheap and efficient electronic data feeds and processing capacity will make it feasible to collect and analyse the data. But cost effective for who? Who benefits from the provision of so much detailed analysis?

In the final analysis it has to be the ultimate owner of the assets or the beneficiary.

- The portfolio manager should be able to improve his own operating efficiency armed with comparative industry data.

- The plan sponsor can take more effective decisions on the disposition of the fund with effective management information.

- The beneficiary can feel more confident that the fiduciaries involved in the fund are being monitored effectively.

Provided the knowledge is correctly handled then it can be said that in the performance measurement sphere knowledge is power.

Customised benchmarks

Introduction

The more widespread use of performance measurement for funds leads, inevitably, to more diverse universes. Within pension funds the different maturities of funds, different cultural, legal and accounting frameworks, and different objectives and risk tolerances widens the spectrum of fund characteristics.

The use of a peer group universe as a benchmark becomes much more problematic in such circumstances. The universe will have to be more tightly defined if it is to offer a true peer comparison and thus provide a benchmark against which useful analysis can be achieved.

This chapter examines some of the implications of these developments and assesses what solutions are likely to be forthcoming.

Index benchmarks

In general the evolution of index benchmarks as described in Chapter 2 has followed investment practice. Thus increasing flows into international markets led to the development of international index series. This trend is continuing and as international investment becomes more widespread and involves more markets and more asset classes so benchmarks will evolve to allow comparison.

Passive investment policies, seeking to match an index benchmark, demand that the benchmark represents a genuine investable opportunity set. Increasing refinement is likely to occur, therefore, as these requirements are met.

Furthermore the ancillary information required, capitalisation, dividend, earnings data for example, will push the various international security exchanges into more rigorous reporting disciplines for the companies quoted. There will also be pressure to conform to internationally accepted standards both as to company data and reporting time scales.

Ultimately the performance measurer will have a comprehensive range of indices available representing most of the asset categories in which investments are held. In most equity markets the tendency will be for a further sub-division of the index into size band and industrial or economic sector along the lines shown for the FT-SE-Actuaries series in Chapter 2.

Style and factor indices

Just as basic market indices followed the trends in international investment there is likely to be a development of indices based on different classifications of companies to reflect portfolio management methods.

Already in the USA portfolios are being managed by specified characteristics other than the more common one of size. Companies are classified by such characteristics as dividend yield, earnings growth, capital gearing or profits cyclicality. Portfolios in their turn are structured along specialist lines to reflect these characteristics. In order to measure the management performance in such portfolios it is necessary to create a benchmark. We are therefore likely to see specialist benchmark indices created which reflect these portfolio styles. Alternatively the performance measurers will create peer group universes of portfolios which have common style or factor characteristics. These universes will themselves be used as performance benchmarks.

Figure 14.1 shows an example of a style analysis carried out by Bankers Trust in the USA as part of their BT – Compare Service. The US equity holdings are analysed to provide a profile categorised by size and by value/growth as shown in the top two charts. The average exposure to these characteristics is plotted over time and shown in the bottom two charts. (The factor exposures used are calculated by BARRA.)

This sample fund has a clear bias towards size but tends to track within the 'core' band in its value/growth emphasis. A look at the upper chart shows that this 'core' outcome is the result of holding stocks at both ends of the spectrum and not from holding 'core' stocks. (Core is classified as falling between –0.10 and +0.10 which actually represents well under 10% of the market value of the equity portfolio).

Further analysis looks at the individually managed portfolios and the returns achieved compared with a universe of portfolios with similar style characteristics.

Figure 14.2 shows the output of such analysis. The overall fund has three managers all with a large company bias, confirming the result in Fig. 14.1. Two have a value bias and one a growth bias. The overall result for the fund, for the

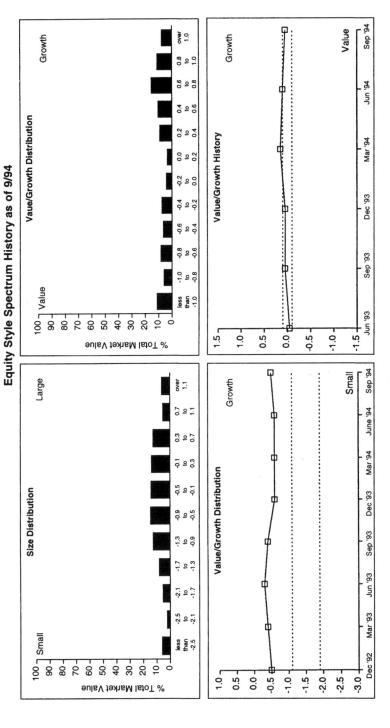

14.1 BT Compare Service – style analysis, ZYZ Master Trust.

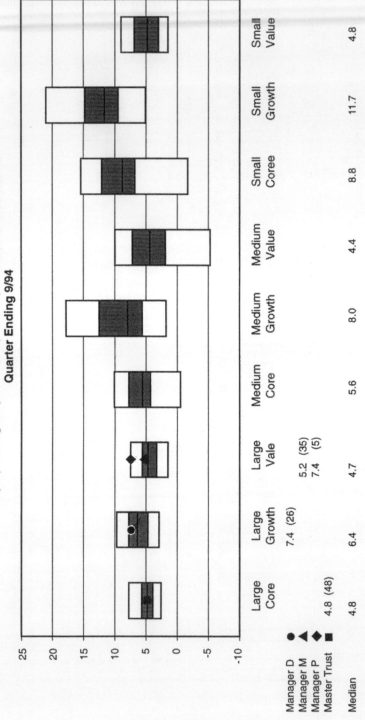

14.2 BT Compare Service – manager analysis, XYZ Master Trust.

particular quarter illustrated, shows that the return was in line with the universe median for 'Large Core' portfolios at 4.8%. (The percentile ranking is shown alongside.)

At the portfolio level manager (D) has outperformed the 'Large Growth' universe while the managers of the 'Large Value' portfolios (M&P) have also outperformed their universe. For this fund the other categories are not represented but median returns for the universe are shown.

Similar analysis can be carried out for the bond portfolios with the categories defined by maturity, duration and coupon. Managers who anticipate interest rate shifts by changing the duration of the portfolio are also characterised.

In addition to style characteristics the equity portfolios can also be analysed by other characteristics such as portfolio beta, R squared and standard error and the returns compared with portfolios with similar values for these variables.

Fund-specific benchmarks

Despite the availability of such a wide range of specialised index benchmarks and universe benchmarks the growing disparity of funds will lead to a demand for customised benchmarks. This will apply particularly at the overall fund level. We are already witnessing a trend towards establishing fund specific benchmarks designed to reflect the unique asset allocation which will meet the fund's liabilities. This trend will accelerate as pension funds become more mature and define the time profile of their liabilities more accurately. Performance measurement relative to such a benchmark will provide information on how well the fund is meeting its performance requirements but will provide no information on the performance of the portfolio managers. This will still need to be supplied by comparison with index or universe benchmarks or customised asset class benchmarks.

These are likely to evolve as a result of more closely defined operating targets. For example an asset class index benchmark may be the basic starting point but volatility and specific risk criteria may be set within which the portfolio manager is expected to operate. Measuring the performance of the portfolio manager operating under such target constraints can only be done against a customised benchmark, or a very carefully constructed peer group universe. Such universes may evolve if a number of funds with sufficiently similar characteristics can be grouped together as shown for the Bankers Trust example.

A further development which will serve to differentiate funds is the introduction of tactical asset allocation (TAA), currency overlay strategies (CAS) and various forms of portfolio insurance (PI). These all tend to be fund specific in operation and the measurement of the overall fund performance will need to take account of the constraints and strategies associated with them. Portfolio insurance in particular is likely to be a cost on the fund which would detract from performance when compared to other funds not operating such a plan. How do you account for the downside protection afforded by such strategies and evaluate the success or failure relative to the sacrificed return?

TAA strategies may operate on a pro-active basis, with the manager responsible for shifting the fund's exposure away from the strategic benchmark, or on a reactive basis with the manager restoring the fund to its benchmark if it strays beyond specified bounds.

In either case the bounds are likely to be specific to the fund and a customised benchmark will be required. Peer group universes will be more difficult to construct but might still be valid if the constraints or bounds are sufficiently similar to allow *useful* comparison.

Conclusion

As funds adopt more complex structures the scope of performance measurement broadens. Coping with new instruments (even where these are customised over-the-counter swaps for example) is a constant challenge.

Establishing satisfactory objective benchmarks and calculating analysis will depend not only on the development of performance measurement techniques but also on the establishment and acceptance of suitable standards across investment frontiers.

The issues

As information, and the processing capacity to handle it, increases there is a danger of over-kill in the performance analysis process. As we have remarked before, the performance measurement process tends to follow fund management practice rather than lead it. If fund structures or management instruments become more complex the ultimate owners of the funds will have an even greater need for accurate performance reporting. The key factor must be that the performance analysis process properly captures and reflects the fund management process. A style analysis of the fund may be of limited value if the management decision process did not identify style as a characteristic of stock selection and portfolio construction.

If there is concern at the complexity of performance analysis it should also be directed further up the chain to the fund management process. A potential cause for complaint against the performance measurement practitioners is that they have failed to establish whether or not increasingly complex fund structures have benefited the funds. As a zero-sum game in aggregate, all incomes generated in fund management, brokerage, etc, must ultimately be met from the investment funds.

Some developments, such as index futures, may facilitate cheaper fund management but the ultimate benefits to the fund of other developments are less obvious.

Performance analysis may be in danger of becoming too complex but it is the management process which must be addressed if we are to return to a more simple structure.

The international dimension

Introduction

As cross border investment becomes more widespread and a larger proportion of portfolio investments are held in non-domestic assets the process of performance measurement becomes more complex. We touched on the evolution of performance standards within some of the major markets in Chapter 7 but extending these standards across national boundaries presents further problems. Moreover the very process of performance measurement is not universally accepted on the same basis as it is in the Anglo-Saxon cultures. Secrecy and confidentiality may be more important than transparency and accountability in some countries while the attitudes to investment return and risk can be very different depending upon the cultural and legal environment.

This final chapter looks at some of these issues, more with a view to airing potential problems than to providing solutions.

International standards

Chapter 7 outlined the evolution of performance standards with particular emphasis on the USA and the UK. Even within these two areas there are variations in the standards which have emerged.

In general there are fewer problems with technical standards. Basic rules as to what constitutes a price, an exchange rate, etc, are agreed and most algorithms for calculating indices, returns, etc, are subject to only minor variations. In most cases the investment communities have reached common agreement amongst themselves as a result of international interchange and the common interest of the participants.

This can really only be said of the simplest of portfolios however. As was discussed in Chapter 6, there are many areas outside the mainstream of investment where pricing standards, for example, are non-existent. Performance measurers, whether they be independent or within the portfolio management organisation, have tended to set their own standards. Thus the rate of return on the same fund can be different when calculated by two different measurers.

For the most part these differences are minor and, provided they remain within acceptable bounds, there is little incentive to pursue the establishment of agreed standards to that level of detail which would eliminate them altogether.

The checks and balances within the market are likely to ensure that reasonable conformity is achieved. For example many funds now have their assets held and valued, for accounting purposes, by independent custodians. They are also likely to have their assets valued, for return reporting purposes, by their fund manager and an independent performance measurer. Although differences can, and do, occur between these three sources of valuation and return data they are unlikely to be tolerated if they are anything other than very minor. A slightly different price used because of different sourcing, marginally different treatment of accrued income or a different algorithm for treating cash flow timing can all lead to a different end figure.

The process of agreeing and enforcing a common standard across all users may be far too complex and costly relative to the benefits to be gained from eliminating these minor differences. Thus there is limited likelihood that agreed international standards of all detailed aspects of performance measurement will materialise in the near future, if ever.

This applies even more with respect to commercial standards. As discussed in Chapter 7, the evolution of the current standards recommended by AIMR in the USA was the result of the cultural, legal and commercial environment in the USA. Whilst the underlying aims and objectives might be embraced as being worthwhile in other countries the detail may not be relevant or practicable in a different legal and commercial framework.

In establishing their committee on standards the EFFAS recognised that what is acceptable in one country may not be so in another. Whilst their objective is to establish global standards where possible the chairman of the committee, Dugald Eadie, recognised that the implementation and policing in individual markets must take account of the structure and traditions of each market.

This is particularly relevant in the area of commercial standards where the legal framework may be in conflict with the standards. Even within the USA the acceptance of the AIMR standards has been far from universal. How much more difficult therefore will it be to agree and implement standards on an international basis, when even the basic concept of measuring performance at all is still in its infancy.

International status of performance measurement

Before we can achieve internationally accepted performance measurement standards we must first achieve the international acceptance of performance measurement, or more particularly the public dissemination of the results.

Performance measurement, as developed in the USA and the UK for example, serves two main purposes.

- As an audit of the progress of the invested assets for the benefit of all interested parties, be they portfolio managers, plan sponsors or ultimate beneficiaries.

- As a management information tool to assess the efficiency with which assets are being managed relative to a set target or benchmark.

Implicit in this process is that the information is made available to the interested parties and, in most cases, to a wider public. Indeed it is to ensure proper and fair disclosure of such information that much of the presentation standards of both AIMR and the NAPF is aimed.

Not all markets would accept the desirability of such explicit information and its dissemination, however. Confidentiality may feature high on the list of priorities in some markets. Thus although the individual investors may seek and get performance measurement on their assets this may only come from the manager and comparative data may be unavailable.

The range of uses and potential benefits of performance measurement are thus limited.

In a translated report by a 'Committee on Investment Performance Evaluation' in Japan the benefits of having pension funds' performance measured was strongly endorsed. It also emphasised that such performance information is highly confidential and its use must be subject to a set of strict rules to respect such confidentiality.

In other countries the very basis of performance measurement may be subject to question. The concept of total return based on the change in market values and income received may not fit in to the legal and cultural framework of the country. In particular where accounting rules dictate the basis of pricing assets other than at market price the total return calculation may be at odds with accounting convention.

Good performance may be represented by the absence of any losses on book cost rather than relative performance against an index or benchmark. This still implies that the performance of the assets needs to be measured but it is likely that different algorithms will apply and different analysis of attribution and risk will be required to meet the circumstances.

The issues

Performance measurement has evolved in response to investment developments and the demands of the participants in the market. Technology has facilitated more timely and detailed analysis to meet these demands and foster new ones. Different markets have evolved at different rates and the demands of investors have varied in the light of their own cultural, legal and commercial environment. In so far as there are certain basic components to any valuation and performance measurement process – asset prices, exchange rates, etc, – there has emerged a trend towards universally accepted formats and standards. These may not have been formally codified but such variations as exist in practice are relatively minor.

Other standards are much more local in application. What is likely to emerge is not a set of international standards but a set of national standards which are relevant to that market and are accepted as such internationally.

Index formulae

The three most commonly used index constructions are the price weighted arithmetic, the price weighted geometric and the capitalisation weighted. Algorithms for each of these are given below, with an indication of well known indices associated with each.

Price weighted arithmetic index (e.g. Dow-Jones)

$$I(t) = \frac{\sum\limits_{i=1}^{n} P_i(t)}{D(t)}$$

where:

$I(t)$ = Index level at time (t)

$P_i(t)$ = Price of constituent shares at time (t)

$D(t)$ = Divisor at time (t)

The Divisor initially would equal the number of shares in the index but would be adjusted for capital changes within the constituents such that:

$$\frac{\sum\limits_{(i=1)}^{n} P_i(t)\text{pre} - \text{change}}{D(t)\text{pre} - \text{change}} = \frac{\sum\limits_{(i=1)}^{n} P_i(t)\text{post} - \text{change}}{D(t)\text{post} - \text{change}}$$

Price-weighted geometric index (e.g. FT Industrial Ordinary 30 Share Index)

$$\frac{I_{(t)}}{I(t-1)} = \left[\frac{P_1(t)\times P_2(t)\times ---\times P_n(t)}{P_1(t-1)\times P_2(t-1)\times ---\times P_n(t-1)}\right]^{\frac{1}{n}}$$

where

$I(t)$ = Index level at time t

$P_1(t)$ = Price at time of constituent share 1

$P_2(t)$ = Price at time of constituent share 2

Market capitalisation weighted index (e.g. S&P 500), FT–SE – A Series, FT– A World Index)

$$I(t) = \frac{\sum\limits_{i=1}^{n} N_i(t)\times P_i(t)}{D(t)}$$

where

$I(t)$ = Index level at time t

N_i = Number of shares in issue of constituent companies at time t

P_i = Price of constituent shares at time t

$D(t)$ = Divisor or Base level at time t

The divisor initially would be a value which solves I(t) to a suitable base value (e.g. 100 or 1000). Subsequently the divisor would need to be adjusted to take account of capital changes in the constituent companies. Unlike the price-weighted arithmetic index only capital changes which affect the total capitalisation of the company need be taken into account. Thus a scrip issue does not affect the divisor but a rights issue does.

The general rule for adjustment of the divisor is:

Adjustment = Last price [(total number of shares now in issue x adjustment factor) – previous number of shares in issue] where the adjustment factor represents the adjustment to historic prices required to maintain comparability with current prices.

187

For example:

Current price = 300p

Shares in issue = 300m

Rights issue terms: 1 for 4 at 260p

Theoretical ex-rights price $= \dfrac{(4 \times 300) + (1 \times 260)}{5}$

$\quad = 292\text{p}$

Adjustment factor $= \dfrac{292}{300}$

$\quad = 0.9733$

Adjustment $= 300\text{p} \, [(375\text{m} \times 0.9733) - 300\text{m}]$

$\quad = \pounds195\text{m}$

This equals the amount of new capital raised i.e. 75m shares × 260p = £195m.

The new Divisor or Base level is thus:-

$$D(t) = D(t-1) \left[1 + \frac{Ct}{\sum\limits_{i=1}^{n} N_i(t-1) \times P_i(t-1)} \right]$$

$$D(t) = D(t-1) + \frac{C(t)}{I(t-1)}$$

Where $C(t)$ = value of capital change which is deemed to take place after the close of trading on day $(t-1)$ and before the calculation of the index day t.

Extract from 'A Practical Approach to the Measurement and Analysis of Investment Performance', Dugald M Eadie, *The Investment Analyst*, December 1973

Performance analysis

Investment decisions have been classified in a number of ways, but it is generally accepted that the decisions are taken at various levels, and that at each level there are elements of selection, allocation and timing. Thus, for a portfolio invested in the UK, the levels might be:

Level 1: UK equities, fixed interest or property.

Level 2: Sectors within each Level 1 category.

Level 3: Individual investments within sectors.

In practice, the dividing lines between the decision levels and the elements of decision are not clear-cut. For example, a decision to hold 60 per cent UK equities and 40 per cent fixed interest is both a selection and allocation decision at Level 1, and it has a timing element if it represents a change in the previous policy at Level 1. Equally, a decision to invest in a specific UK equity stock may be taken without previously considering its impact on the Level 2 decision. Nevertheless, the divisions do exist, however implicitly, in any investment decision-making process.

The examples below demonstrate how the notional fund concept can be applied to distinguish the contributions to performance from any of these decisions.

The principle underlying the examples is that the actual achievements of a fund are compared with the results that could have been expected if a number of alternative decisions had been taken. Each such comparison gives a contribution to performance, which is expressed as a percentage of the mean fund so as to provide an analysis of the internal rate of return (IRR). For example, one such comparison is between the actual fund and the initial fund, with no voluntary transactions being carried out. The result of this comparison is a measure of the effect of dealing on the actual fund's performance. Other comparisons involve notional funds, whereby the actual investments of the fund are 'mirrored' by hypothetical investments in a share index. A simple example of such a comparison is the selection contribution, being the difference between returns from actual stocks held and those resulting from hypothetical investment in the appropriate sector indices.

The examples illustrate some of the possible comparisons, displayed in a manner which makes it practical to assimilate the information. The approach may be used to monitor any of the investment decisions outlined above, but the examples are restricted to the timing of UK Equity/Cash allocation decisions, the allocation and selection of sectors within UK equities, the selection of stocks, and the timing of stock purchases and sales.

Example 1

This example is concerned with Fund G, which has a long-term policy of 100 per cent investment in UK equities. The manager, however, has discretion to go 'liquid' when he chooses. Table A2.1 gives a summary of the analysis of relative performance, with all the numbers in 'basis points' or hundredths of a per cent. Example 2 gives a full explanation of the construction of the 'mini-All Share Index', and of the first three columns of the analysis. Finally, the Building Materials sector is examined in detail in Example 3.

Over the year to 30th October 1973, the mini-All Share Index return was –4.45 per cent, or –445 points. (See Table 3.2.) Table A2.1 gives, at the bottom right-hand corner, a total relative performance for Fund G of +415 points, showing that the fund almost broke even in absolute terms. The relative performance can readily be analysed from Table A2.1, the key points being as follows:

1. The initial fund, if left untouched, would have been 270 points down on the index.

2. The dealing activity during the year has improved the performance dramatically, particularly in the Building Materials sector (+360) and Cash (+215).

Table A2.1 Fund G – Performance analysis – 31/10/72–30/10/73

Sector	Index	Loading	Initial Portfolio Policy	Selection	Total	Dealing	Grand Total
Building Materials	+32	0	+32	-205	-173	+360	+187
Wines and Spirits	+115	-115	0				
Chemicals	+27	+14	+41	+62	+103		+103
Oil	+56	-19	+37	+110	+147		+147
Life Insurance	-230	-92	-322	-25	-347	+110	-237
Cash						+215	+215
Total	0	-212	-212	-58	-270	+685	+415

The initial fund analysis is explained more fully in Example 2. The dealing figures are constructed by running a notional fund, invested in the mini-All Share Index, and comparing in detail the achievements of the actual investments with those of the notional fund. Thus, the +215 for cash dealing reflects the fact that, during the year, money has been invested in cash at a time when the Index was considerably higher than at the year-end. Relative to the Index, this cash investment was therefore well-timed.

It should be noted that, for this type of analysis, the approximation of dates becomes more dangerous. Since the index can move by several percentage points in a few days, the new money inputs can be incorrectly valued in the notional fund which is being used as an overall standard. The solution is to concentrate on the relatively large new money inputs, but perhaps with a lower threshold to define 'large'.

Example 2
This example is concerned with the allocation decision at Level 2 within UK Equities. Table A2.2 gives details of the construction of the mini-All Share Index consisting of only 5 sectors. The contribution made by each sector to the All Share return of –4.45 per cent is shown in 'basis points', or hundredths of a per cent, and the relative contribution is also shown, being the excess return of each sector, multiplied by its weight in the index. This final column emphasises the fact that Life Insurance is the major detractor from the performance of the index, the other four sectors all giving positive performance relative to the average.

Table A2.3 gives the details of Fund G, which is fully invested, but has a 'loading' or allocation on 31st October, 1972 which differs from the standard set by the index.

The performance contributions to Fund G due to the sector loading decisions are calculated by constructing a notional fund which has the same allocation as

Table A2.2 Mini–All share index

Sector	% Index 31st Oct 1972	Return on Index	Contribution to All Share	Relative Contribution
Building Materials	15	-2.3%	-35	+32
Wines and Spirits	10	+7.0%	+70	+115
Chemicals	20	-3.1%	-62	+27
Oil	30	-2.6%	-78	+56
Life Insurance	25	-13.6%	-340	-230
Mini-All-Share	100	-4.5%	-445	0

Table A2.3 Fund G – sector contributions – 31/10/72–30/10/73

Sector	31st Oct,1972			Cont's to Fund G Perf.		
	% Index	%Fund G	Load Ratio	Index	Loading	Policy
Building Materials	15	15	100	+32	0	+32
Wines and Spirits	10	0	0	+115	-115	0
Chemicals	20	30	150	+27	+14	+41
Oil	30	20	67	+56	-19	+37
Life Insurance	25	35	140	-230	-92	-322
Total	100	100	-	0	-212	-212

Fund G but achieves the sector index returns. The selection contributions, as shown in Table A2.1, are then determined by comparing the actual performance of the initial investments in each sector with the sector notional fund.

The loading column in Table A2.3 gives a clear analysis of the effect of the allocation decisions. The decision to stay out of Wines and Spirits completely has cost 115 points, or 1.15 per cent, while the above-average loading in Life Insurance has cost 92 points, or 0.92 per cent.

The other decisions have had little impact, and the total effect is a loss of over 2 per cent. This example illustrates the fact that, if the objective is to out-perform the All-Share Index, the allocation of investments between sectors is an important decision level to be monitored. In particular, it should be noted that the omission of a sector may be just as risky as the heavy commitment of money to a sector.

Although Example 2 described a situation with no new money or cash flows, the same principle can readily be applied to a dynamic situation. If there has been new money during the period, the initial loading contributions can still be calculated exactly as above, but expressed as a percentage of the mean fund so as to give their contributions to the IRR. Also, as is demonstrated in the next example, the actual impact of portfolio changes including the investment of new money can be determined using the notional fund concept.

Example 3

This example concentrates on the Building Materials sector in Fund G. The fund holds two stocks in the sector on 31st October, 1972, and during the year adds to the holding of one, while switching the other to a third stock. Table A2.4 tabulates this information, and in addition illustrates the impact of the dealing activity. Note that the appreciation on the initial holdings is separated from that on transactions. This allows the dynamic impact of changes to be identified, and it is instructive to note that the well-timed sale of Glynwed is a major contributor.

Although Table A2.4 displays the Buildings Materials sector information in cash terms, it is a straightforward matter to compare each result with what could have been expected in either the mini-All Share or Building Materials index.

For example, the initial sector valuation of £2945, if invested in the Building Materials index, would have lost £68 over the year. The actual loss of £470 implies a relative loss of £402, which, when divided by the mean fund, leads to the Selection figure of –205 in Table A2.1.

Similarly, the transactions for the sector amount in total to a net investment of £1135 on 1st May, 1973. The performance of this net investment in practice is compared with its hypothetical performance in the mini-All Share Index, the result being a cash relative gain of £707, or +360 basis points as in Table A2.1.

Table A2.4 Fund G – building materials stock contribution

	Valuation 31st Oct 1972	Appreciation	Net Investment	Dealing Profit	Valuation 30th Oct 1973
Glynwed	1,630	-180	-2,290	+840	0
Pilkington Brothers	0	0	+2,290	+80	2,370
Tarmac	1,315	-290	+1,135	-110	2,050
Total	2,945	-470	+1,135	+810	4,420

Transactions

22nd Aug, 1972	Sell 1,000 Glynwed at 229p
	Buy 662 Pilkington at 346p
1st May, 1973	Buy 500 Tarmac at 227p

One final point emerging from this example is that any attempt to analyse the performance without considering portfolio changes can easily lead to error. Although a large institutional portfolio may have a relatively low total turnover, it is quite likely to have major turnover within individual sectors. An analysis of Fund G which ignored dealings might conclude that the Building Materials sector had not performed well, whereas in fact the dealings have given the sector an excellent performance.

Practical application

These three examples were designed to illustrate different aspects of the performance analysis which can be produced using the notional fund concept. In practice, the analysis for a UK equity fund would use the FT-Actuaries All Share Index, with its 41 sectors. The calculations, though based throughout on simple algebra, are best performed on a computer.

The market data required consists of the adjusted prices of the stocks involved at the beginning and end of the period, the dividend data for these stocks, plus all necessary index values. The fund data is extracted as a by-product of a routine valuation process. For such a process, the normal updating information required would be:

Stock Name

Number of shares bought or sold

Consideration (to update book cost).

The only additional information required for the performance analysis is the date of each transaction. The information on cash flows and balances is often a difficulty, but the data processing system can at least identify all cash movements resulting from investment activity, leaving only the new money flows to be isolated.

By using a 'building brick' approach, working up from individual transactions, the summary information of the type shown in Examples 1 and 2 can be produced without further manual effort.

Also, the computation of the internal rate of return is an automatic by-product, while the notional fund can be used to estimate the time-weighted rate of return using the approximation suggested by the Investment Analysts' Working Group.

Extract from 'Measuring the Impact of Future and Options on Investment Portfolios; A South African Perspective', Adrian C Ryder and Heather D McLeod

Illustration of performance calculation methodologies

An example has been developed to illustrate the various calculation methodologies. Returns are typical of the 1990 year. Purchases, sales, income and end market value have been constructed so as to achieve the desired performance in each asset class.

Assume that the portfolio was hedged by selling futures contracts at the start of the year, effectively reducing equity exposure from 65% to 55%. The calculations in respect of the futures contracts are shown below.

Price beginning: 4000

Want R10m hedge $\therefore \dfrac{10\ 000\ 000}{4000 \times 10} = 250$ contracts

Initial margin of 2000 per contract = R0.5 million

Price ending: 3130

Profit on futures = $(3130 - 4000) \times 250 \times 10 - 1 = $ R2.175 million

Table A3.1 Physical portfolio

	Market Value Beginning Rm	Purchases Rm	Sales Rm	Income Rm	Market Value Rm	Annual Performance End
Equity	65	3.25	0	3.25	61.575	-5.3%
Property	10	1.00	0	1.00	11.500	15.0%
Bonds	20	2.40	0	2.40	22.000	10.0%
Cash	5	1.00	0	1.00	6.000	20.0%
	100	7.65	0	7.65	101.075	1.1%

Additional income earned on futures profit $= 1/2 \times 2.175 \times 20\%$

$$= RO.218 \text{ million}$$

'Cash' method

In the cash method, the profits on the futures are treated as an increase to cash income. The additional interest earned on the futures profit is also an increase to cash income. This results in increased purchases of cash assets.

Table A3.2 Cash method

	Market Value Beginning Rm	Purchases Rm	Sales Rm	Income Rm	Market Value Rm	Annual Performance End
Equity	65	3.250	0	3.250	61.575	-5.3%
Property	10	1.000	0	1.000	11.500	15.0%
Bonds	20	2.400	0	2.400	22.000	10.0%
Cash	5	1.0 + 2.175 +0.218	0	1.0 + 2.175 +0.218	6.0 + 2.175	67.9%
	100	10.043	0	10.043	103.468	3.5%

'Asset class' method

In the asset class method, profits on equity futures are allocated to the equity asset class. The profit results in inflow to the portfolio and is thus treated as a sale in the equity asset class. The additional interest on the futures profit is treated as cash income. These two items result in additional purchases of cash assets.

Table A3.3 Asset class method

	Market Value Beginning Rm	Purchases Rm	Sales Rm	Income Rm	Market Value Rm	Annual Performance End
Equity	65	3.250	2.175	3.250	61.575	-2.0%
Property	10	1.000	0	1.000	11.500	15.0%
Bonds	20	2.400	0	2.400	22.000	10.0%
Cash	5	1.0 + 2.175 + 0.218	0	1.0 + 0.218 + 0.218	6.0 + 2.175	20.0%
	100	10.043	2.175	7.868	103.468	3.5%

'Total' method

In the total method, performance in each asset class is calculated on the physical assets only. A single adjustment is made at the end of the calculation to include derivatives in the total portfolio. The profit on futures is treated as a sale as money flows into the portfolio. The additional interest on the futures profit is treated as income. Additional balancing purchases are made.

The cash method allocates all profit on the futures position to the cash class, reasoning that margin at SAFEX is a cash item and all profits have come through this cash account. This produced a return on cash of 67.9% when the market return was 20.0%. This is patent nonsense and the method can readily be discarded.

The 'asset class' method allocates profit on the equity futures to the equity asset class. Performance on equity is thus –2.0% compared to the market return of –5.3%. The cash performance is unaffected and remains at 20%. This method is the intuitive one chosen by portfolio managers but its use raises some difficult philosophical issues as discussed under 'The methodology dilemma' below.

Table A3.4 Total method

	Market Value Beginning Rm	Purchases Rm	Sales Rm	Income Rm	Market Value Rm	Annual Performance End
Equity	65	3.250	0	3.250	61.575	-5.3%
Property	10	1.000	0	1.000	11.500	15.0%
Bonds	20	2.400	0	2.400	22.000	10.0%
Cash	5	1.000	0	1.000	6.000	20.0%
	100	10.043	2.175	7.868	103.468	3.5%
After Futures	100	7.650	21.175	7.650	101.075	3.5%
		+ 2.175		+ 0.218	+ 2.175	
		+ 0.218			+ 0.218	

The total method reports performance in each asset class as if only physical assets were present and makes a single adjustment to the total portfolio. The portfolio performance is thus similar to that of a portfolio made up of 55% rather than 65% equity. The British recommendations produce the same result although using a much more complex means to arrive at the answer.

The methodology dilemma

The dilemma in choosing between the asset class and total methods is not easily resolved. The problem is further illustrated below.

Assume a portfolio with 65% in equity and split-funded between three portfolio managers. The trustees issue an instruction to reduce equity exposure to 55%, leaving the managers to choose how this is to be accomplished.

Manager 1 sells physical equity, he reports equity performance of –5.3%.

Manager 2 buys ELFI Bears, he reports equity performance of –2.0%.

Manager 3 sells futures, he reports equity performance of either –2.0% or –5.3%, depending on the methodology adopted.

All three managers, have achieved the same effect and all three will obtain the same total performance, not allowing for anomalies in the pricing of the various instruments.

We believe there must be neutrality of treatment and that the same equity performance should be reported for all three managers.

The recent British recommendations in this regard treat futures philosophically as asset allocation tools. In other words futures affect the allocation between asset classes and do not contribute to the result in any particular asset class. This results in an equity performance of –5.3% for all three managers in the example.

To follow the British philosophy locally would imply using the total method or the British equivalent for futures. An adjustment would need to be developed to the way in which ELFIs are treated to ensure consistency.

The American philosophy is different. The widespread usage in the US of specialist portfolio managers has lead to a fundamentally different accounting treatment in portfolios. The industry standard, mandatory from 1993, is to allocate all new cash flow amongst the equity, bond and property classes. Cash is not a separate asset class but may form part of any of the other classes, thus there is equity-cash, bond-cash and property-cash. The decision to lighten up on equity in the portfolio would result in a performance of –2.0% being reported in the above example for all three managers.

The American philosophy follows the asset class methodology as far as futures are concerned. However, current South African practice is to keep cash as a separate class (or amalgamated with bonds) and thus Manager 1 will report –5.3% while Managers 2 and 3 report –2.0%. If the principal of equivalence of treatment is accepted, this difference in reporting is unacceptable.

Index

Printed and bound by CPI Group (UK) Ltd, Croydon, CR0 4YY

11/05/2025

01866607-0002